SELF PRESERVATION

ANITA YOUNG HALLMAN

Deseret Book Company
Salt Lake City, Utah

Library of Congress Cataloging-in-Publication Data

Hallman, Anita, 1958–
    Self preservation / by Anita Hallman.
        p.   cm.
    Includes bibliographical references and index.
    ISBN 1-57345-230-0 (pb)
    1. Autobiography—Authorship. 2. Biography as a literacy form.
    I. Title.
    CT25.H35   1997
    808'.06692—dc21   97-2130
                                                                           CIP

Printed in the United States of America   18961

10   9   8   7   6   5   4   3   2   1

To my dad,
Elmer Richard Young

CONTENTS

Types of Film
Processing and Developing
Environment
Storage
Handling and Treatment
Negatives
Color Slides
Refrigeration of Photographic Materials
Damage Repair
Oldies
A Few Final Hints

The Wrong Materials
The Perfect Scrapbook
Cautions and Hints
Getting Organized
Types of Scrapbooks
Creative Ideas
Avoid Burnout
Storage

Inventory List
Labeling Relics and Heirlooms
Where to Keep Keepsakes
Enjoy Your Keepsakes
Care of Heirlooms
Natural Disasters
Woods and Furniture
Metals
Glass and Ceramics
Books
Textiles
Cleaning Textiles
Storing Textiles
Leather
Framing Artwork, Certificates, and Heirlooms
A Keepsake Box
Creating Your Own Heirlooms

ACKNOWLEDGMENTS

This book is my response to hundreds of people who have heard me give presentations and asked, "Why don't you write a book?" Over the past fourteen years I have spoken to literally thousands of people and tried to motivate them in organizing and keeping records. I hope this book will be a useful resource for them and others like them.

I've been able to "rub shoulders" with archivists and learn from them as I compiled the histories for the Primary and Relief Society General Boards for several years. Over the years I've visited with many conservators and experts and am grateful for the knowledge they've shared with me. I've also learned from the audiences I've addressed. Thank you for your tips.

There are many specific people to thank in connection with this book. First, my thanks to Marielen Christensen for the inspiration she gave me in organizing my records into different areas. She and her husband, Anthony, have been experts in the area of scrapbooks longer than anyone I know. A heartfelt thanks to Kelli Rencher Rollins for her years of pushing me to get my lectures into book form. Her continual faith and advocacy of this project have been very encouraging. Bob Ligget offered dedicated and tireless support; he has been the motivational fire under me to get this done. Thank you, Bob, for patiently helping me with the determination I needed.

To my "experts," a *huge* thank you! Dave Young helped so much with the Audio and Video chapter. He kept me current. To Rodger Newbold for his photographic expertise—thanks for answering *every* question I kept having. Thanks to Gary Shellabarger, for sharing his vast knowledge of computers and genealogy; to Bill Ormond, who knows more about textiles than anyone I know; and to Joan Young, for her editing, her help on definitions, and most of all for her listening ear.

Thanks to Emily Watts, my editor, for helping my words look good on paper, and to Kent Ware, my designer, for his artistic eye. And thank you to Deseret Book for having confidence in this project.

A special thanks to my family and friends, who gave me such great support and inspiration and who helped and played with my children so I could sit at the computer quietly. To my wonderfully patient children, Ceciley and Joseph (and one on the way). Ceciley, your sincere prayers that Mom would get her book done were so appreciated. Most of all, I thank my best friend and partner forever, Joe. He's been the best critic, editor, info-finder, baby-sitter, and all-around Good Guy there could be.

This book is dedicated to all my family. To those who have lived before me: thank you for the heritage you bequeathed to me. To all my relatives who are sharing life on this earth with me now: You are the best. And to all my family not yet living: May you know through my records who I am and that I love you.

WHERE DO I START?

If you are like I was years ago, you have photos, certificates, and important letters and documents all over your home. I had scrapbooks of all kinds put together with poor materials that were falling apart. Genealogy and family history sheets were thrown into a box. We had filmed many hours of home videos but never labeled them adequately; it was nearly impossible to locate the taping of a specific event. Basically, things were a real mess. Once, when I needed my husband's birth certificate, it took me hours to find it in the chaotic jumble of our records. I was frustrated! Such events finally sparked me to straighten out my "stuff."

Eight Areas of Preserving Memories

When I decided to get organized, it seemed natural to divide my personal and family records into eight different areas:

Journal
Personal History
Family History
Book of Remembrance/Genealogy
Photographs
Scrapbooks

1

Keepsakes and Heirlooms
Audio and Video Recordings

These categories make sense to me because there is an obvious distinction between them. Each covers a part of our lives a bit differently, though some may overlap. You may choose to arrange things in a different way, according to your own individual style. Perhaps you will divide your records into just two areas—or you may have ten. The essential thing is not how you categorize your records and memories but that you do something—anything—to preserve and organize them!

Before you get into specific details, there are some basic, general things you need to know about materials and procedures. Chapter 2 contains important information on papers and other archival materials that you'll want to familiarize yourself with before you proceed with any of the other areas. Chapters 3 through 10 cover the eight areas I have listed, offering some "how-to" ideas and encouragement for each category. And Chapter 11 ties the eight areas together by showing ways to preserve your memories using a home computer. An appendix gives addresses and numbers of suppliers and places to go for more information.

Some of the information in this book may seem technical or far above what you can do. Don't be overwhelmed. *Just do the best you can!* It has taken me years to get my records together, and I'm still working on them. Simply take one area at a time, doing what you can do and what works well for you.

Preserving memories should not be an awful chore. It can be a wonderful highlight in our lives as we make lasting ties with previous and future generations. I've always felt that if we're not having fun, we're doing it wrong. As you discover what works for you, you will find that record keeping can be fun.

Why Keep Records?

Perhaps the best way to start your record-keeping adventure would be to gain a personal testimony of the importance of what you're doing. There are many reasons why we should prepare and preserve family records. When we realize the benefits, keeping records becomes enjoyable, satisfying, and fun. It also becomes easier for us to do. Here are some reasons that motivate me.

Our posterity will know us. When I read about my ancestors, I feel close to them. I understand and appreciate their lives and experiences. Without their own written histories, I would know little about them. Some of my ancestors have left no history at all; sadly, they are little more than names with a few vital statistics to me. I don't know anything else about them. It doesn't take very many generations for people to be forgotten if no history is left behind. Who were they? What were their feelings? What did they like to do? What do we have in common?

I have descendants of my own, and hope to have more someday. I want them to know me! If I leave them a personal record of my life, they can know me in ways that they otherwise wouldn't be able to. President Spencer W. Kimball promised: "As our posterity read of our life's experiences, they, too, will come to know and love us. And in that glorious day when our families are together in the eternities, we will already be acquainted" (*Ensign*, December 1980, p. 60).

You are the link that ties the past and the future together. Think of how important your role is in giving continuity to your family's traditions and stories. Are you a strong link or a weak one?

We receive helpful insights and perspective to deal with trials and problems we face. A poignant truism is that "those who do not learn from the past are destined to repeat it." Learning how our ancestors endured and overcame their challenges will help us as we work through our own. We can also learn to tolerate and maybe even be happy with our trying circumstances. When we read, for example, that Grandma had health problems and was still happy, or that Grandpa had a bad case of acne and yet lived through his teen years just fine, we know that we can do it too, even with our shortcomings. And perhaps the records of our own lives will likewise help and give support to future generations.

3

I once read that journals and histories preserve not only the memories of everyday life, but also the wisdom and insight of ancestors. Much of what we have learned from our family can become lost as we progress through life—wisdom, customs, traditions, talents. Through records, this knowledge becomes immortal, and a future relative may expand upon it rather than have to reinvent the wheel.

Records can help us with what I call a "reality check." When I was serving as a Young Women's president, the Beehives were acting immaturely one night, or so I thought. Later that week, however, I was reading in my journal about when I was a Beehive. I was more out of control than they were! It was so good for me as a leader to realize that they were just acting their age. I became much more sensitive and tolerant of their lives and feelings.

Another "reality check" occurs for our own children when we keep records. As our children grow up and read from our records, they will believe that we were young once too. Every once in a while my mom will mention her high school days, maybe a date she had. This boggles my mind! My mother, dating?! Soon reality sets in and I realize that of course Mom was young once, and she dealt with growing-up experiences similar to mine. If we keep records, events in our lives (and those of our family members) will be more "real" to us and to our posterity. When we stop to think that our parents and other loved ones have dealt with problems and joys like our own, we become more accepting of their advice to us.

Record keeping is a great source of self-evaluation. We can see our personal growth through it. For example, by reading a year-old journal entry, I can see that I've learned things that I didn't know a year ago. I understand things better now than I did then. With hindsight, I can see and evaluate how I have handled situations in the past and how they could have been handled differently. Similarly, from time to time I recognize, looking back a year or two, some areas in which I was actually ahead then of where I am now. Since I have a built-in desire to be continually improving, my journals motivate me to improve if I find that I have slipped. By reading old journals and records I can learn so much about myself and how I can improve my life. Sometimes I am shocked that I ever thought or felt what I did. I never would have remembered or even believed some of what has happened if I hadn't written it down.

We can learn lessons about life from record keeping. Events and circumstances that I have been concerned about have usually seemed to work out for the best. Looking back, I can see that some trying experience never really was "the end of the world," as I might have thought at the time it was happening. In fact, challenges and problems usually ended up bringing unforeseen blessings. I've learned priorities through record keeping. I've learned, for example, that housekeeping will always be here, but my dad won't. I've learned that life goes by fast, so I should love and enjoy each minute.

Perspective on circumstances and situations can be gained by reading our journals. A dear friend told me that she had to eat many of her words after she had children of her own. By reading her journal from before she had children, she could see that her perceptions of mothering had greatly changed.

Keeping records helps us to see the Lord's hand in our lives. I can see how he has watched over and protected me. Hindsight is a wonderful thing. I often can't see what is right before me, but going back and reading about the past may make the picture more clear. Sacred experiences and miracles in my life become permanent reminders of my testimony and of God's love for me. I know that the strong and precious feelings I have gained from such experiences would be lost if I hadn't written them down. Orson Pratt, an early Apostle, once asked: "How many thousands have been miraculously healed in this church, and yet no one has recorded the circumstances. Is this right? Should these miraculous manifestations of the power of God be forgotten and pass into oblivion?" (*Millennial Star,* 15 May 1849, p. 152).

If we keep our own records, they will be more accurate than if we leave the recording of our life history up to our children. President Joseph Fielding Smith said, "Every important event in our lives should be placed in a record, by us individually" (*Doctrines of Salvation*, 3 vols., comp. Bruce R. McConkie [Salt Lake City: Bookcraft, 1955], 2:204). Years ago I typed up a history that my dad and aunt had written about my grandmother. I'm so glad to have it! However, as I was typing it, I wondered, "Is this *really* how it was, or just how my dad and aunt *perceived* that my grandmother felt?"

Remember, you're the best authority on you! No one else can know your actions, thoughts, and feelings as you can. I can almost guarantee that someday, someone will try to write a history of your life for you if you don't do it yourself. Will they be able to depict it accurately?

Records and histories hold great worth. Thousands of dollars have been paid for important historical documents. Kovel's Antiques & Collectibles has published a list of valuable signatures:

Document signed by Thomas Jefferson: $5,000
Document signed by Napoleon Bonaparte I: $2,800
Cut signature of Abraham Lincoln: $2,700
Cut signature of Wolfgang Amadeus Mozart: $2,500
Cut signature of Daniel Boone: $1,700
Cut signature of Ben Franklin: $1,600

You may think, "Well, I'm not Mozart or anyone else famous; my things aren't worth that much." But there is another value placed on documents, one that isn't monetary. I know a girl whose mother died when she was three months old. When the girl was in high school, her father ran across a journal the mother had kept during her pregnancy and those first three months of the girl's life. There is no price you could give to buy that journal from her. Someday your writings will be valuable to someone, most likely to you! My records are worth so much to me, I could never put a price on them.

Keeping records can become a fun and creative hobby. It is for me and many others.

Much of the history of the world and the Church we

wouldn't know if ordinary individuals hadn't taken the time to write it down. I'm so thankful for those who did. If we're really honest with ourselves, we can all admit that we forget things. Much of the history we learn about in school is derived from ordinary journals and writings of people who have been close to the significant events of their time.

Every year in May the Aaronic Priesthood quorums in our ward have an Aaronic Priesthood commemoration celebration. The Aaronic Priesthood was restored on May 15, 1829. Every year around March 17 we celebrate the founding of the Relief Society, which was organized on March 17, 1842. Have you ever wondered, as I have, why no one ever celebrates the restoration of the Melchizedek Priesthood? The answer to this came to me as I was studying the life of Joseph Smith. We do not celebrate it because we do not know the date of the restoration. We know that it occurred somewhere between May 15, 1829, and April 6, 1830, but we do not know the exact date!

The Prophet Joseph Smith deplored the neglect of record keeping during that historical and eventful period of the Church. Recollection of this oversight always gave him great sorrow. He later said that if he had such historical data in his possession, he "would not part with them for any sum of money; but we have neglected to take minutes of such things, thinking, perhaps, that they would never benefit us afterwards; which, if we had them now, would decide almost every point of doctrine which might be agitated. But this has been neglected, and now we cannot bear record to the Church and the world, of the great and glorious manifestations which have been made to us with that degree of power and authority we otherwise could, if we now had these things to publish abroad" (*Teachings of the Prophet Joseph Smith*, sel. Joseph Fielding Smith [Salt Lake City: Deseret Book, 1976], p. 72).

Although probably none of us will have anything as glorious as the restoration of the priesthood happen to us, our lives are still important. The events and miracles of our lives are valuable

7

to us and our posterity. Let's learn from the mistakes of early members of the Church and record important events.

In 3 Nephi 23:9–13, Jesus reminded the multitudes in America that he had commanded Samuel the Lamanite to testify to them many things. He then asked, "Was it not so? And his disciples answered him and said: Yea, Lord, Samuel did prophesy according to thy words, and they were all fulfilled." Then Christ asked, "How be it that ye have not written this thing?"

How many of us have had prayers answered, blessings and miracles bestowed in our lives, and not recorded them? What will we say if Jesus asks us where they are written?

By consciously recording and preserving our lives, we will have the desire to live better, more meaningful lives. Benjamin Franklin said:

> *If you would not be forgotten*
> *As soon as you're dead and rotten,*
> *Either write something worth reading,*
> *Or do things worth the writing.*

We want events to be recorded in heaven. Elder Hartman Rector Jr., a member of the First Quorum of the Seventy, gave a wonderful devotional address at Brigham Young University entitled "Roots and Branches." Elder Rector quoted Doctrine and Covenants 128:6–7 to demonstrate the importance placed on record keeping by the Prophet Joseph Smith. Then he stated that sometimes we get the idea, "Well, it won't make any difference whether it's recorded here, because it's recorded in heaven." Don't be so sure, he says.

"Now, the nature of this ordinance consists in the power of the priesthood, by the revelation of Jesus Christ, wherein it is granted that whatsoever you bind on earth shall be bound in heaven, and whatsoever you loose on earth shall be loosed in heaven. Or, in other words, taking a different view of the translation, whatsoever you record on earth shall be recorded in heaven, and whatsoever you do not record on earth shall not be recorded in heaven" (D&C 128:8).

This revelation speaks specifically of baptisms for the dead and of making sure that they are properly recorded. Elder Rector, however, suggested—as have many others—that it refers to all our personal records as well. "Does that sound as if maybe you'd better write it?" he said. "I think so. If you really want to get credit for it, you'd better write it down.

"I am convinced that it is not what we do here upon this earth that will condemn us at the last day, anyway," Elder Rector went on. "No, because if we do something wrong, we can repent of it, can't we? You see, the Lord Jesus Christ granted repentance to us all. That is not going to hurt us, for those sins will be blotted out. If we did something good, and we record that, we will get credit for it. So you see, it's not what we do, it's what we don't do that we're going to have a rough time repenting of at the last day. So we ought to write it. Let's write it down. It is vitally important that we do. And then the record is in heaven" (BYU devotional address, February 10, 1981).

Our prophets have asked us to. Now, if none of the preceding reasons are good enough to motivate you to keep some kind of a record, here's one that should: Our beloved prophet Spencer W. Kimball asked us to. In his words, "We renew our appeal for the keeping of individual histories and accounts of sacred experiences in our lives—answered prayers, inspiration from the Lord, administrations in our behalf, a record of the special times and events of our lives" (*The Teachings of Spencer W. Kimball*, ed. Edward L. Kimball [Salt Lake City: Bookcraft, 1981], p. 349). That's good enough for me.

There are many benefits in keeping records. One that I have seen in others is a big boost in self-esteem. When your life is in front of you in a scrapbook or history, it brings such satisfaction. My children have loved looking at their scrapbooks, which they call "My Book" from a very early age. They love to point out people they know, favorite clothes, and loved toys in the photos. It's a secure feeling to have records and to see and enjoy them.

Another benefit to my keeping records is the example it is

setting for my children and other family members. Whenever my toddler does something fun or cute, my six-year-old daughter says, "Mom, let's write this in Joseph's journal." I'm also thrilled that she knows stories about her ancestors (and about relatives still living). Her favorite stories are about when her mom and dad were little, and she likes to have them repeated often. She feels a tie with the past when she sees and hears stories about keepsakes of mine. At a very early age, she would often say, "Mom, show me something special." Our family bonds are stronger because of our records.

May I encourage you with all my heart to begin today, if you have not already done so, to create a record of your life. Claim the blessings that are waiting in abundance for you!

THE RIGHT MATERIALS

Preserve: (1) to keep safe from injury, harm or destruction; (2) to keep alive, intact, or free from decay; (3) to keep up and reserve for personal or special use.

MERRIAM WEBSTER'S COLLEGIATE DICTIONARY,
10TH EDITION

Over the years as I have spoken on the subject of record preservation, I have repeatedly been asked the same question: "Why do my materials have to be archival?" The answer is simple: Papers, photos, fabrics, and keepsakes will all suffer some kind of deterioration over the years. That deterioration may be slight or it may completely destroy your valuables, depending on the materials and storage practices used. It's just smart to use good preservation materials and techniques with items you care about. The more acids and chemicals in the environment, the faster the decay.

Picture what happens when you mix two or more incompatible chemicals together. You get a "chemical reaction." We've all seen the chemical reaction that occurs when we mix vinegar and baking soda, for instance. The more incompatible the chemicals are, the more dramatic and perhaps destructive the reaction can be.

All the things we save (photos, cards, letters, programs, tickets, and so on) already have some chemicals and/or acids in them. When we store them together with even more acidic materials, such as notebook pages or cardboard boxes, we cause chemical reactions and speed up the decaying process.

The migration of an acidic material to a less acidic or pH neutral material may occur directly when the two materials are in intimate contact. For example, acid may migrate from a highly acidic cardboard box to a less acidic paper placed in the box, causing harm to the paper.

Obviously, *the less acid we have in our records, journals, and scrapbooks, the longer they will last.* But for papers, simply being acid-free isn't enough. In order for them to really last, they need to have been buffered with an alkaline substance. The most common buffers are magnesium carbonate and calcium carbonate. A paper may be acid-free right after it is manufactured, but over a period of time, residual chlorine from bleaching, aluminum sulfate from sizing, pollutants in the environment, and acid migration can all lead to the formation of more acids. When an alkaline substance is added to the paper, it neutralizes the acids and gives a reserve or buffer for counteracting acids that may form in the future.

My husband has a pair of pants that is full of holes created by contact with auto battery acid. This same process of weakening the organic fibers through contact with a strong acid can ruin your papers, photos, and other treasures over time. On the flip side of this, you know that when you have an acidy, upset stomach, an antacid can help. These generally have active ingredients of calcium or magnesium to buffer your queasy stomach and neutralize the acids there. When you're buying paper, then, look for brands that are both acid-free and buffered.

Archival Quality

Archival, archivally sound, and *preservation quality* are terms that are used very loosely today in referring to preservation materials. Many consumers confuse them with *acid-free* and assume that they mean the same thing. They do not. No standards exist that say just how long an "archival" material will last or how "good" it is. In other words, *archival* is a term that has no reliable measure. It actually means different things to different conservators, depending on what is being preserved.

To a historical museum, *archival* may mean that something has to last five hundred years before any harm is noted. For a schoolteacher, a material may possibly have to last only thirty years to be archival for her needs. When I tried to get a clear definition from the Library of Congress, an expert there told me: "Archivally sound materials will last a long time!" Because there is no standard or measure of time, a manufacturer could advertise that its glue, for example, is "archivally sound." People may buy that glue, thinking it will look good and last forever, only to find that it is made from materials guaranteed to hold without staining or yellowing for just three to five years. But because that might seem to be a "long time" for glue to hold, it can be advertised as archival.

As a side note, the American National Standards Institute (ANSI) has changed the term *archival storage* to *extended-term storage*. This was done because the term *archival* has been interpreted to have so many different meanings, everything from "forever" to "temporary storage of actively used information."

There are some guidelines that help identify if an item is truly archival or archivally sound. Keep in mind again that *archival* is a *nontechnical* term used to describe something that is safely used for preservation or conservation purposes; there is no measure of time governing the definition.

1. Something archival would be durable.

2. Something archivally sound would be acid-free, chemically stable, or neutral pH.

3. Archival quality materials have a strong resistance to adverse environmental conditions.

4. Anything preserved archivally could be removed—meaning that it could be returned to its original condition. (For example, lamination, bronzing, and adhering with some glues and tapes are nonreversible and hence not archival.)

5. An ink that is archival would be permanent. This means the ink would be fade proof, waterproof, and chemical proof.

6. An archival paper or board would be not only acid-free but buffered with an alkaline solution.

One more important thing to know: As with papers, just because an ink is acid-free, it cannot be assumed that it is archival. (Are you confused?) For example, I have some marking pens that are acid-free. However, they are water soluble. This does not allow them to be archival. Water-soluble markers clearly cannot be considered permanent because they will bleed and run.

My best advice is to be very aware of your materials and what they are made of. When I speak of acid-free or archival-quality materials in this book, assume that I am speaking of the highest-quality materials. More comprehensive definitions of terms can be read in the glossary at the back of the book.

Paper

Most of the things we deal with in preservation contain paper. Journals, histories, scrapbooks, and genealogies all require paper. The popularity of desktop computers has moved many personal documents to electronic storage, but even these must be cared for if ever printed out.

If all of our writing were inscribed on stone, parchment, or gold plates, it could last for centuries! Unfortunately (or perhaps fortunately, for that matter) we do not write this way anymore. Before paper was made, parchment (made from sheep or goat skin) and vellum (made from calf, kid, or sometimes lamb skin) were the materials used for documents and books. Parchment and vellum were expensive due to the limited supply of skins and the lengthy preparation required.

The first paper was made in China around A.D. 105. It was composed of pulp from cloth scraps, a technique later adopted by the Europeans. This method for making fine handmade paper, without introducing chemicals, has changed very little over the centuries. Most paper we use today, however, is not handmade.

As literacy increased and the demand for paper grew, it became necessary to find a way to produce paper inexpensively and in large quantities. Manufacturers began to use worn, deteriorated rags for papermaking. They added chemicals, especially chlorine, to bleach the discolored rags. This created papers that were considerably weaker than the quality, acid-free ones. The deterioration over the years of these lesser-grade papers has been shown to be much more dramatic than that of earlier, high-quality papers.

With the Industrial Revolution, ground wood pulp was used as the source of cellulose for papermaking. With the increased production of paper and printing, cotton and linen rags were becoming scarce and costly. Wood pulp was both abundant and inexpensive. By 1885, wood-pulp-based paper had become the most widely used. But a major problem with wood pulp is that it is highly acidic in nature. Also, to keep inks from running, the soft, absorbent wood-pulp paper must be treated with chemicals such as aluminum sulfate and rosin. During papermaking, moisture combines with these chemicals, forming sulfuric acid. The acid slowly breaks down the cellulose fibers in the paper, and the pages begin to fall apart.

Lignin, a component of the cell walls of plants, is often left in paper. It is largely responsible for the strength and rigidity of plants, but its presence in paper contributes to chemical degradation. Lignin deteriorates very quickly in light, causing the paper to yellow and darken. It can be, to a large extent, removed during manufacturing, but is often left in because the removal process adds to the total cost. Most poor-quality papers, such as newsprint and the paper in mass-market paperback books, contain lignin.

The inherent acidity of modern paper is such that many of our precious letters, journals, books, and manuscripts are literally falling apart. Over the past ten years, the public has been demanding better quality, acid-free paper. It is much more widely used today than previously over the past century.

In 1980 the federal government and the papermaking industry formed a committee to set standards for paper permanency. The result was the creation of the Permanent Paper Standard.

This is paper that meets the American National Standards Institute standard Z39.48 1984. According to this standard, to be considered permanent, paper must meet the following requirements:

1. It must have a pH level of 7.5 or higher.

2. It must contain an alkaline buffer of calcium carbonate or another alkaline.

3. It must be free of chemical impurities and contain cotton or rag fibers.

4. It must be resistant to tears and folding.

These standards have led manufacturers to produce higher-quality paper than before. We should take advantage of its availability. It used to be that the only acid-free paper you could buy was white or off-white, but now you can get acid-free paper in any color you can think of—even black. (See appendix for sources.)

It is important to note here that not all acid-free papers are necessarily alkaline or buffered papers. The terms are not interchangeable. *Acid-free* is a general term indicating that the paper has a neutral pH of 7.0 or higher. However, acid-free papers can often turn acidic from environmental conditions or acid migration. To be truly safe, good-quality papers must be both acid-free *and* alkaline buffered.

There are several different ways you can test paper yourself for acidity. An inexpensive pH testing pen is my favorite. Simply write on the paper with it and follow the instructions to see what color to look for. One kind of pen with a chlorophenol red indicator solution turns purple on paper with a pH of 6.5 or higher. Another pen contains Bromcresol green, a bright green chemical ink that changes color from blue (acid-free) to green (some acid content) to yellow (high acid content) when applied to paper. Also available are easy-to-use pH indicator strips. Place them on the paper, add a drop of distilled water, and then check the color. See instructions for color interpretation. Other kits, testers, and meters are available at a higher cost, but they really aren't necessary for basic home use. (See appendix for sources.)

16

Environmental Problems with Paper

Light. Light, especially ultraviolet rays from sunlight and fluorescent lights, is one of the most common destroyers of paper and other organic materials. Have you ever seen a newspaper that was left out on a driveway during a hot, sunny afternoon? The part that was facing the sun will be yellowed. Or have you ever placed leaves on dark construction paper and left them in the sun? The paper not shielded by the leaves fades, leaving a print. This is a fun childhood activity, but it may also help in illustrating that the paper is actually being damaged by the light. This is what will happen to our valuable records over time if we leave them exposed to light.

Atomic-sized, energized particles called photons are found in light. These stimulate chemical reactions in paper, resulting in its deterioration. Light causes changes in the structure of the paper itself, causing paper to discolor as well as dry out and become weak and brittle. Exposure to light also bleaches and fades many types of inks. Those especially susceptible are watercolors, felt-tip pens, iron gall inks, and certain inks made from dyes. Unfortunately, once damage from light is done, it can't be reversed.

Heat generated by light is harmful as well. It dehydrates the cellulose fibers in paper, causing them to lose their lubricant-like resiliency. Heat-damaged papers can literally crack apart in your hands. Incandescent light doesn't have much ultraviolet radiation, but it generates intense heat.

An easy solution is simply to keep valuables away from light. (You'll be reading that often throughout this book.) Use blinds or curtains to restrict intense sunlight. Ultraviolet filters can be used on windows and fluorescent lights to eliminate ultraviolet radiation. Use low-wattage, incandescent bulbs (60 watts or lower) around your valuables, and store things at least four feet away from the bulbs.

Temperature and humidity. High temperature, humidity, and moisture wreak havoc on paper. Chemical reactions occur that lead to embrittlement and discoloration. Too much moisture accelerates oxidation and causes mold and mildew. Moisture also stimulates chemical reactions that produce acids. When paper becomes moldy and water-stained, it becomes weak. This allows tears and rips to happen more readily. Moisture also causes inks to run or bleed.

On the other hand, too little humidity causes paper to become dry, brittle, and dark in color. Changing temperature from hot to cold or humidity from dry to humid is called *cycling*. This is very detrimental to paper fibers. Cycling creates an enormous stress on the fibers as they absorb moisture and swell, then dry and contract in response to the changing moisture or temperature. The Library of Congress suggests that the optimum temperature for paper is 68 to 70 degrees Fahrenheit and that the ideal relative humidity is between 45 and 55 percent.

Many kinds of hygrometers, desiccants, and silica gel canisters are available to help you regulate the humidity in your storage areas. These absorb moisture caused by excessive humidity. They are priced anywhere from $5.00 to $175.00, and come in many different styles. The tiny packets of silica gel will absorb moisture but will not measure the humidity for you. Be careful to not get your papers too dry when using them. (See the appendix for places to buy them.)

Keep your home well ventilated with air-conditioning and heating systems. Filters should be changed often to combat the invasion of dust and soot. Use common sense as to where you keep your valuables. For example, if you have a heat vent under your bed, don't keep your journal right there. Don't keep a valuable certificate on a wall that receives direct sunlight a lot of the day.

Pests. We all would like to think that we will never have any rodents, insects, termites, cockroaches, or similar "critters" in our basements, attics, or garages, but it happens to the best of us. I've seen valuable old letters that were stored in a shoe box in a basement ruined because mice had nested in them. Insects and rodents can easily eat through stacks of paper. Paper that has been exposed to such pests often has little holes and dark spots (droppings), which are acidic. General rules of housekeeping can help, but another good rule is to keep your valuables in your living areas. I've never had a family of mice or bugs living in my bedroom, but I have in my unfinished basement! Avoid storing papers in any area that is warm and damp—these conditions encourage little pests. Avoid having any food or beverages around your valuables that will attract "critters." Check periodically to see if there has been any sign of them. If a chronic problem is present, contact an exterminator or spray the area—NOT YOUR VALUABLES—with insecticides.

Pollutants. Car exhausts, all kinds of smoke (tobacco, burning wood, and so on), and atmospheric pollution—especially sulfur dioxide, hydrogen sulfide, and nitrogen oxide—all create problems for paper. Paper exposed to pollutants will become weak, brittle, and stained. Household products such as solvents, aerosols, and paints with fumes have a deteriorative effect on paper as well. All these pollutants produce destructive acids and accelerate oxidation. Even oils from our hands leave smudge marks and help promote deterioration. Use cotton gloves when handling old or precious papers, and avoid storing them in any area where pollutants exist.

Ink

What you choose as a writing instrument may cause damage to your written documents. I have journals from high school on which I used a pen with four different colors. I thought that pen was so neat at the time! However, now the green writing has faded and is hardly legible, and the red and blue have bled. My husband has scriptures that were underlined in blue ink—the ink bled and the other side of the page now shows purple underlining. I have seen journals with this same problem, and they are unreadable.

To be archival, inks must be resistant to light, heat, and water (so as to not fade, bleed, or smear). Inks must not contain any impurities that would affect the permanence of paper. They also must not deteriorate with time. For example, iron gall ink contains iron sulfate, oak galls, and arabic gum, and is acidic. It fades to brown and eventually burns through paper. Many water-soluble pens fade very easily.

The three qualities to look for in an ink are (1) chemical proof or acid-free, with a pH above 7.0; (2) fade proof, meaning that the ink won't discolor over time or when exposed to light; and (3) waterproof, meaning that it won't smear, bleed, discolor, or fade if it comes in contact with any moisture. Inks with these three qualities are often called "permanent."

A carbon or pigma ink is best. Carbon ink is found in accountant, archival, legal carbide, laundry, or permanent pens. Pigma inks are made from pigments that don't bleed. Inks made from dyes tend to bleed even without the presence of water.

In the past, permanent pens have typically been black. Recently they have also been made in colors. I'm still of the opinion that black is the best and should be used on all important documents. Black will photocopy much better than another color as well. If you still have a typewriter, like I do (the last of a dying breed), then use one with a carbon ribbon.

Copies made from a laser computer printer are permanent. The ink is set in with heat. Generally, ink-jet copies are light resistant but not water resistant. They are permanent if they remain dry, but will run if they get wet. Documents generated by a dot matrix printer are not permanent; I have seen such copies fade quite fast. Stamp pads can safely be used if inked with a permanent, archival ink.

In short, it is important and easy to use ink that is permanent: fade proof, waterproof, and chemical proof or acid-free.

Fasteners and Adhesives

I have personally ruined many things by using the wrong kind of glue or tape. Rubber cements or any other "smelly" glues will discolor paper, photos, and fabric. Masking tape and cellophane tapes are damaging over time. Staples and paper clips can bend, cut, discolor, and damage.

To be considered truly archival, any kind of mounting must be reversible. This means that the object can be removed from its mount without being damaged. Following are detailed descriptions of various types of fasteners.

Glue. What you need to look for is a glue that is water soluble and pH neutral. A safe glue will be reversible when moistened with water. With a water-soluble glue I can usually pull the glued item off even when the glue is dry, but if it's a bit stuck, I just wet a cotton swab and moisten under a corner or edge as I ease my way under. When gluing a paper, there is no need to plaster the whole page. That usually results in a crinkly appearance anyway. Simply dab a bit of glue on the corners or around the edges.

A good water-soluble glue stick is made by Avery Dennison. Elmers School Glue is also water soluble and safe. (It has to be the School Glue; normal Elmers is not as good. I guess the School Glue is made safe because the elementary school kids frequently eat it!)

If a glue smells like rubber cement, is oily, or can't be washed off your hands with water, it's obvious that it is not appropriate to use for preservation purposes. Use a pH testing pen to check for acidity. Simply let some glue dry on an acid-free paper and test it with your pen. However, even if a glue shows no acids on a pH test, it can still be oily and cause stains.

Pure-grade wheat paste is one of the finest adhesives available. Many conservators will not use any glue but this. You can make it easily yourself with the following recipe. (See appendix for where to buy wheat starch.)

Microwave Wheat Paste
1 tablespoon wheat starch
5 tablespoons distilled water

Place the wheat starch in a deep container, add distilled water, and place it in the microwave oven. Microwave on a high setting for 20 to 30 seconds, remove paste, and stir. Place it back in the unit and microwave another 20 to 30 seconds. Remove it and stir again. Repeat this process for 3 to 4 minutes (depending on the power of your microwave), until paste thickens. Paste should stand for a few minutes after microwaving before you use it.

Tapes. Acid-free tape is available for paper. Again, it's important to note that one of the requirements for something to be archival is for it to be able to be returned to its original condition. Whatever you do needs to be totally reversible, without damage to the object. Even some acid-free tapes can rip paper.

Cellophane and masking tapes are corrosive and non-reversible, and they leave a permanent, translucent or brown-colored residue of adhesive. Cellophane tends to dry out, lose its adhering properties, and turn yellow in a short time. 3M's #850 Transparent tape is an archival adhesive. Since it is acid-free, it can be used on papers, but it is hard to get it off (if you need to) without ripping the paper. 3M's #415 double-sided film tape is great for encapsulation (see below), but use caution in taping something you may want to remove easily.

Filmoplast, linen, and acid-free paper tapes can be reversed in water. These are neutral pH and safe for use on paper. They come in a wide variety of types and sizes. Some are transparent and some are not. They can be used for book repair, document mending, hinging, and frame sealing. (See appendix for sources.)

The monetary or historical value of a document should determine the type of tape used. Any document of great significance should be mended with Japanese paper and starch paste. Talk to a conservator for proper techniques and instruction.

Corners. Acid-free mounting corners are simple to use. Items can obviously be removed easily from them, since they don't actually stick to the mounted item. Use caution in using them with brittle or fragile papers, however. They may place too much stress on a fragile corner and cause it to tear. Be cautious in removing an item so you don't bend or put stress on it.

Staples, clips, and bands. Metallic paper clips and staples can oxidize (rust) in high humidity, leaving reddish-brown stains. If a clip is needed, use a plastic one, which won't rust or discolor paper. Be careful, though, since it can still bend and perforate the paper. Staples leave holes, and paper clips cause creases, scratches, and perforations. In high humidity, rubber bands will soften and stick to paper. In low humidity, they will dry out and leave a hard, dark-brown residue that sticks to paper. In high humidity, even string can become acidic and leave brown lines on paper.

A caution about adhesives. When an item is very valuable, fragile, old, or has sentimental value, I choose to use no adhesives at all. Although there are "safe" adhesives, I feel that any adhesive has the potential to possibly age an item or make it difficult to remove. Documents can be placed through slits in a mounting paper to hold them in place. Or an original document can be stored in an archival folder, box, or sheet protector without adhesives; copies can be made for everyday viewing.

Photocopying

Items that are deteriorating can be photocopied onto acid-free, buffered paper. Make sure that the copy machine uses a powdered toner, not a liquid one. The powdered toner is heat-set in and will be permanent. If your local copy center doesn't have acid-free paper to copy onto, most places don't mind if you bring your own. It's a good idea to photocopy valuable documents such as diplomas and birth, wedding, and death certificates. Newspaper articles and other fragile articles can be preserved well with a photocopy. Copies of these valuables can be kept in a safety deposit box or given to a family member living outside your home. This is good insurance in case your original is ever damaged or destroyed.

Deacidification

A deacidification spray such as Wei'T'o or Bookkeeper spray can be used on important documents and papers to keep them from becoming yellow and aged. One treatment with the spray can convert acidic, unstable paper into stabilized, permanent paper that can last three to four hundred years. The spray neutralizes the attacking acids on the paper that cause embrittlement and yellowing and eventual disintegration. Spraying an item won't restore it to its original condition and reverse the damage already done, but it will prevent it from getting any worse. The sprays deposit a buffering agent on the paper that will also neutralize the effects of harmful acids in the atmosphere and counteract against future acid attacks. Follow the instructions on the individual product can. Spraying is good for artwork, journals, newspapers, and certificates.

Newspapers pose big problems for preservation. The paper is acidic and of poor quality; it also contains lignin, which causes it to yellow and darken. Many newspapers, however, contain things we want to keep. One way to save articles is to photocopy them onto acid-free paper; an advantage to this idea is that you can shrink the article as you copy it, making it more easily accessible. I often photocopy newspapers onto an off-white paper that resembles newsprint. This makes an item look more like the original.

Another alternative for storage is to wash and deacidify the newspaper. Simply put your article in a glass baking dish and slowly pour in distilled water to cover it with a depth of about an inch. Let it soak for fifteen minutes. If the water is really yellow, change it and repeat the process. Pour out the water and carefully lay the article out flat to dry. If it is a large article, use a fiberglass or polyester window screen to support the weight of the paper. Wash it with the distilled water in the bathtub or a small, clean wading pool. Once the article is dry, you should deacidify it with the W'eiT'o or Bookkeeper spray. This will keep it from yellowing any further. Whenever I save a current newspaper article, I spray it right away to keep it from going yellow and brittle in the first place.

Newspapers that have been deacidified can be stored in

archival folders or boxes made their size; they can also be rolled with Mylar (see page 27).

Encapsulate, Don't Laminate

I love to laminate posters and handouts. It makes them washable and durable. However, lamination isn't a good treatment for valuable papers and documents. Paper needs to breathe, and it can't when it's sealed in plastic. Also, lamination uses heat and adhesives. These bond with the chemicals in paper and produce acids, which in turn cause papers to discolor and deteriorate. The plastic used in lamination is chemically unstable as well. To me, one of the biggest drawbacks of lamination is that once something is laminated, the process can never be reversed.

Encapsulation is a method developed by the Library of Congress as a way of protecting paper items from the perils of handling and pollutants while at the same time making the items available for viewing. Although it sounds technical, it's really quite easy. Follow these simple instructions.

1. Cut two sheets of Mylar one inch larger on each side than the size of the document being saved.

2. Place the document on one sheet of the Mylar and place a heavy object on it to hold it in place.

3. Apply 3M's #415 double-sided tape to the Mylar around the edges, not touching the document. Be sure to leave a space about ¼ to ½ inch between the tape and the edge of the document. Keep a corner or two free from tape so that the article can "breathe." Any moisture that is already present or that may develop can escape from those openings.

4. Peel away the paper backing of the tape and remove the object holding the document in place.

5. Carefully align the second sheet of Mylar on top of the bottom sheet.

6. With a soft cloth, apply pressure to the top sheet along the strips of tape to seal it.

7. Trim the edges and round off the corners, if needed.

This process is totally reversible. A document can be taken out of the plastic simply by cutting open an edge of the Mylar.

If it is not important to be able to be see both sides of an item, you might want to encapsulate it on a single side. This gives the item the look of being framed. It is also beneficial in giving fragile items additional support. Place the item on an acid-free paper or board. Apply the tape to the board as in steps 3 and 4 above. Place the Mylar on top and continue as indicated for regular encapsulation.

I've also seen encapsulation done by sewing around the edges of the Mylar with nylon thread on a regular sewing machine.

Before encapsulating any article that is acidic, you should deacidify it first.

Proper Storage

Store valuable documents in quality protectors. Papers should be stored in acid-free, buffered envelopes or folders, polyester (Mylar), polyethylene, or polypropylene sheet protectors, acid-free boxes, or metal filing cabinets or boxes. NEVER store important papers in plastics that are acetate or made from polyvinyl chloride (PVC). Keep them out of ordinary cardboard boxes, paper sacks, envelopes, and wooden boxes or drawers. Wood contains tannic acid and formaldehyde, which are damaging to paper. (Note that hard woods such as oak and walnut are not as porous as soft woods such as pine, and don't have as many wood by-products. They are still acidic, but they are safer than soft woods.) Many ordinary cardboard boxes and sacks are acidic and contain lignin or water-soluble dyes that can cause harm to paper.

When storing clippings, newspaper articles, or other documents, isolate those that are not acid-free from other papers to avoid acid migration from one to the other. Simply keep each document in its own acid-free, buffered envelope or folder.

Old letters are often in bits and pieces because they fall apart where they have been folded and creased. Folding weakens the fibers in the paper, and it eventually tears along the crease. (You've seen how a paper is torn easily after it has been folded and creased.) Unfold all paper items and lay them flat. Letters can be stored with their envelopes, just not in them.

Documents and papers that are large can be rolled instead of folded. An archival piece of Mylar can be rolled together with the paper to protect it. Paper can also be rolled and stored in or around an acid-free, buffered tube. Tubes can also be lined with acid-free, buffered paper or a polyester (Mylar) film. The tube should be at least 3 inches in diameter. If the item is stiff, use a bigger tube. Interleave buffered tissue paper as you roll the document, making sure that it is covered with tissue to the end. Tie the tube with cotton twill tape to keep it from unrolling.

Garages, attics, and basements are not good storage places for valuables. They are often homes to mice and other little pests. The fluctuations in temperature and humidity are too great there as well. Unfinished or damp basements and garages may cause mold or mildew. Basements are also subject to broken water pipes and other flooding. Garages have monoxide gases and other pollutants that are harmful. The best storage space for your precious things is in your main-floor living areas.

None of us can find or create storage that will guarantee absolute protection against a natural disaster. However, a little common sense can help. For example, my sister moved to Houston during a time of terrible flooding there. She wisely decided that all her records and valuables should be stored on the top floor of her home. If you don't have a two-story home, store your valuables at least one foot above the floor. This will help protect them against possible flooding. Store things away from water pipes, air-conditioning units, radiators, windows, skylights, and fireplaces, and do not put them directly against an exterior wall.

A fireproof box is a good place for some of your valuables. (See more on fireproof boxes in Chapter 7 on photographs.) A safety deposit box is another "safe" idea. Make copies of particularly valuable documents and give them to a family member

27

living in another city. (Remember that whole cities have been destroyed by floods and fire.)

Damage Control

The best damage control is prevention. Purchase smoke alarms and fire extinguishers for your home. Carbon monoxide alarms can also be helpful. Follow the instructions above for storage and proper care of papers. Take care of a problem when it is small; for example, mend a small tear before it becomes a big tear.

When you are in doubt about treating *anything,* do nothing. Place the damaged item in a protective envelope or sleeve and contact a conservator for advice. This may save you from doing something wrong and causing more damage.

No matter how careful you are or what you do, you still may find yourself with damaged papers. Following are some suggestions for minimizing loss.

Water. If paper has been the casualty of a flood or other water damage, recovery may be possible. Paper will react to high humidity or water in a number of ways. Inks and paints will blur and run, adhesives will weaken or totally give, dimensions may change, and the paper will become stained. Pieces of stacked, wet paper or pages of a book will most likely stick together. Mold growth and insect infestation are also dangers.

One of the dangers of wet materials is that they are extremely fragile. Never move them until you have a plan of action and a safe place to put them. However, you don't have much time to save them. Think fast.

Mold starts to grow on wet paper objects within forty-eight to seventy-two hours, so temperature and humidity should be controlled as soon as possible. Set up fans to keep air circulating. Remove any wet things that may contribute to the high humidity level, such as water-logged carpet.

If damage is severe, or you don't know quite what to do, immediately freeze the papers. Any document that is printed on coated paper or one with running or blurred ink should be frozen immediately. Freezing puts the papers in a state of limbo, keeps mold from growing, and prevents ink from additional running. This gives you some time to prepare for how you will handle the papers. A professional disaster recovery service or a conservator can help recommend how the papers must be dried when you take them out of the freezer. Make sure that you dry them under the direction of a specialist. Freezer drying, vacuum thermal drying, or vacuum-freeze drying are the preferred techniques for frozen documents. You will need help and advice in doing these.

To prepare papers to be frozen, place waxed paper between individual sheets. Bundles of these papers alternated with waxed paper can be wrapped in freezer paper.

If freezing is not an option, you must start air drying as soon as possible. Never iron papers to quicken the drying process. Set up your drying area where there are open windows and fans to keep the air circulating continuously. Place a single page on a clean, flat surface between two absorbent paper towels. If the paper is really wet, you will need to change the towels frequently. You can place a flat object (such as a book) on top so that the paper won't curl while drying. If you don't have enough space to lay out single sheets, you can make small stacks with white paper towels or unprinted newsprint placed between the papers.

Dirt and mud. Mud and sewage can be gently rinsed off a paper object while it is still wet. Dry dirt can be removed by using a soft camel's-hair brush or a powdered eraser. Only try to clean paper yourself if it has a firm surface. You can make a powdered eraser by shredding a white vinyl eraser into crumbs with a cheese grater. Pour the powder on the paper and gently rub it with clean fingers or a soft brush. The powder will loosen the dirt and then you can brush away the residue. Do not attempt to do any sort of major treatment yourself. Call a conservator. Conservators can also reduce oil and grease stains with solvents.

Mold. A musty smell can be an indication of the presence of mold. If papers smell musty, remove and isolate any pages that have spores or mold. This will help keep the mold from

29

spreading to other papers. Brush the mold with a soft brush to remove spores. Avoid brushing toward yourself or other valuable materials. If the mold is extensive, consult a conservator.

Some sunlight is recommended for killing mold or mildew if the paper is moist or dry, not wet. However, be careful not to leave it in the sun for an extended period, especially if it has suffered light damage already. A professional may be able to kill the mold with chemicals.

Rips and tears. An archival document-repair tape can be used to fix damage such as punctures or tears. Archival tape will not yellow or become brittle with age. It has a neutral pH adhesive and is reversible with water or common mineral spirits. (See the discussion of tapes on page 22.)

Fire. In a fire, smoke deposits carbon residue in a greasy film over both sides of the paper. Only a conservator can safely clean this film off without surface abrasion and permanent staining. Obviously, if the item has actually been burned, there is not much that can be done—an argument again for storing copies of valuable papers outside your home.

By following the guidelines given earlier in this chapter, you can avoid many disastrous problems with your valuable papers and documents. All it takes is a little time, care, and common sense.

Now that you know the basics about materials and storage procedures, you're ready to carry out the grand adventure of preserving your memories!

JOURNALS

"Anyone who holds the journal of an ancestor can testify of the joy in possessing it."

SPENCER W. KIMBALL

Many of our most cherished moments would be lost if we didn't record them in our journals. Journals are a wonderful place to record meaningful insights and to preserve our memories. They are a tremendous vehicle for recording our spiritual and emotional growth. They also serve as a valuable link between generations.

People often ask me why and how to keep a journal. Although there could be entire books full of answers to those questions, this chapter will give some guidelines and "helps" to start you on your way to being a consistent journal writer.

Why Keep a Journal?

In Chapter 1, I outlined many reasons for keeping records, and you might want to reread those with journal keeping in mind. There are a few other things, though, that seem to relate specifically to journals.

Keep the Lord in remembrance. President Spencer W. Kimball was a strong advocate for keeping a journal. On many occasions he encouraged Church members to keep personal journals and family records. In the December 1980 *New Era* he said, "Those who keep a personal journal are more likely to keep the Lord in remembrance in their daily lives." When I first read this, I thought, "Well, how could that be so?" I didn't see the connection. However, I now see that it is true in my own life. (As if I needed to question a prophet!) My journal is not only a record of my feelings but also an accounting of the day, an evaluation of what I have done and how I am progressing in my life. It wouldn't be very fulfilling to write, "Today I robbed a bank, yelled at the neighbors, or was rude to my mother." How awful! I want to be able to write good things, so I tend to try to *do* good things. *It is true that the more consistent I am in my journal writing, the more I think of the Lord in my daily life.*

Great catharsis. We've all heard the old adage that when we are upset with something or someone, we should write our feelings in a letter and then tear it up. The same principle works here. Our journals can become a great catharsis. They help release emotional pressure. Theologian C. S. Lewis kept a journal following the death of his wife, Helen Joy Lewis. The journal became his emotional salvation as he recorded his struggles with grief. Many who are trying to cope with grief themselves have felt great comfort through reading his writings.

I worked for several years as a counselor to troubled youth in elementary schools. Many of these children bore the burdens of difficult family life, poverty, and other troubles. It is nearly impossible to positively motivate a child when you know little of the sources of his or her problems, frustrations, and unacceptable behavior. As a counselor to these children, I found that having them write to me in a private notebook let them reveal emotions that they would never vocalize. I learned much that I otherwise would not have known. When I required the students to write something down, they had to truly search to find out what they were really thinking and feeling—and why. This insight and understanding helped me to help them, as it also helped them to help themselves. The same will be true for us: By writing, we can understand more clearly what we are experiencing.

President Kimball didn't say this, but *I* feel that by asking us

32

to keep journals he was giving us our own prescription for dealing with stress. Keeping a journal is an excellent release of emotion. How much better our lives would be if we could unleash pent-up anxieties by writing rather than reacting with anger or engaging in other counterproductive behaviors. By keeping a journal, we can find peace and clarity in the midst of crisis or change.

Good funeral material. Okay, this does sound a bit morbid, but it is really a good idea. My sister-in-law spoke at her mother's funeral and did a lot of reading from her mother's journal. It was wonderful motivation! If chosen wisely, journal excerpts can be the most powerful things said at the funeral.

We've been asked to. I had the wonderful opportunity of meeting President Kimball at his home. He gave me and my husband a kiss. It was a magical five minutes. As I left his home, I just happened to say, "Oh, I have such an exciting thing to write in my journal today!" He looked me straight in the eye, pointed his finger, and said, "And you *are* keeping a journal, aren't you?" After that, how could I not! He has asked each of us to keep records and journals. Follow his guide and "Do it!"

What Should I Write?

Facts and feelings. Every once in a while, evaluate your writing to see if you have a good balance of feelings and facts. Both are important to have and to remember, but sometimes our journals are full of just one or the other.

Some journals record only emotion. Some people tend to go to their journals primarily when they are deeply depressed or highly elated. These are good and important times to write, but what about the average day? We should write about average days, too, since they make up the majority of our lives and tell more accurately who we are. If we were to leave out the feelings and events of average days, our journals (and our lives) would appear as emotional roller coasters, rather than fairly smooth highways that contain a few hills and valleys.

Some journals are full of only facts, with hardly any feelings at all. I was guilty of this when I was young. I have old diaries that contain University of Utah basketball scores from the sixties. My diaries were full of: "I went to school, played with Chris, and ate dinner . . ." But how did I *feel?* Facts and feelings mixed together make for more interesting reading and show the whole person. My sister Joan said that she was reading an old journal from the time before her twins were born. She was amazed at how much she could accomplish in those days (facts), and how her perspectives (feelings) on things have changed. Find balance with both facts and feelings and check yourself every once in a while to make sure that you include both.

Love for others. It is important to tell of the love you have for family members and friends. There was a man who went on several missions for the Church and held many prominent civic positions. When he died, his family went to his journals, seeking to feel close to him. (If you have lost someone, you probably know that feeling.) A common, effective method of working through the mourning process is to search through writings, possessions, and mementoes of a lost loved one. This may reestablish emotional ties and provide evidence of that person's love. In this case, however, it didn't work. Not once in his many, many journals did this man mention his family or his love for them. His journals were full of his missionary and civic experiences. Those experiences were tremendous and should have been written about, but not at the expense of leaving out loved ones. That family felt quite empty.

By contrast, I once heard of a young missionary who was killed by a train while on his mission. His journal was full of his feelings for family and friends. His mother went through his journal and photocopied these paragraphs and gave them to the individuals he was writing about. It was an incredible experience for her and for his friends.

You might want to put a running table of contents in the front of your journal that includes references to your special entries about others. For example, if I wrote: "Feelings for Joe,

June 19, 1980," then you or anyone else could quickly find an expression of my feelings for my husband, Joe.

A caution for when you write about other people: Make sure that feelings are expressed honestly and factually, but don't write descriptive details that could hurt, embarrass, or incriminate another. Never write gossip or confidential information that should not be someone else's business. For example, my husband is currently serving as a bishop. It would be inappropriate for him to record in his journal the details and names associated with confessions or problems that others bring to him. His journal should be something that I could read.

Service. Many people are afraid to tell in their journals all the good things they do each day. They feel that they are not being humble or are not serving in secret or with the right attitude if they record it. *It's okay to write it!* In fact, I feel you *should* mention what good you do. First of all, the world will not be reading your journal. It is a personal thing that most likely only you or a very few people will read while you are alive. After you are gone, it still won't be open to everyone. But what a wonderful example of service you can give your posterity! When I read of all the good things my ancestors did, it inspires me to want to do the same.

In the December 1980 *New Era,* President Kimball gives us advice on what to write:

"1. Your journal should record ways you face up to challenges that beset you. Experiences of work, relations with people and an awareness of the rightness and wrongness of actions will always be relevant. Tell of problems as old as the world and how you dealt with them.

"2. Your journal should contain your true self rather than a picture of you when you are 'made up' for a public performance. There is a temptation to paint one's virtues in rich color and whitewash the vices, but there is always the opposite pitfall of accentuating the negative.

"3. The truth should be told, but don't emphasize the negative. Even a long life full of inspiring experiences can be brought to the dust by one ugly story. Why dwell on that one ugly truth about someone whose life has been largely circumspect?"

How Often Should I Write?

Personally, I think that the best journals are kept daily. Events and emotions are fresh on your mind when you record them every day. I like to write at the end of the day; it becomes a great source of wisdom and insight to me regarding how I have spent the day. Did I waste a lot of time? Did I do my "daily good deed"? Writing becomes a measuring stick of accountability to myself and to God. There have been times when I have had trials or frustrating circumstances in my life. There have also been many wonderful, exciting, and spiritual times. Often these situations are over, cleared up, or figured out in a week or so. If I had waited a week to write about them, the powerful emotions that I was feeling while they were happening would have been tempered. Once trials and frustrations are settled or worked out, we see them in a different light. Exciting, happy experiences also mellow with time. The power and warmth from a spiritual experience is lessened. When we describe them at a later date, the details and sparkle are often lost. What makes trials a teaching tool is to read how we feel *right as they are happening,* as well as how we feel later when they are resolved.

Some people have a hard time writing every day and write less frequently. I think, however, that we should try to write in our journals at least once a week. I have a hard time remembering details beyond a week. If you don't write at least that often, your work turns into more of a history than a journal.

I searched everywhere I could to find some guide or direction as to how often we should write. I found countless passages that said to pray daily and to read your scriptures daily. But with record keeping, everything said simply to keep records. A lady once announced to me, "Oh, I keep my journal, it's in a box in my closet; I won't give it away, I will always keep it!" I've laughed about that a lot. We need to do more than just "keep" or "possess" a journal. The best admonition that I found on how often to write in your journal was from President Kimball when he said, "Your story should be written now while it is fresh and while the true details are available."

Whether you write daily, weekly, or even less frequently, the most accurate journals in terms of content, facts, and feelings are written as soon as possible after significant events occur.

How Much Should I Write?

How much to write is a personal decision. Each of us lives with his or her own unique set of circumstances, is in a different stage of life, and has a different amount of time available for writing. At times I have written more and at times less than I do now. I have seen two very different ends of the spectrum. I have a friend who buys calendars with big squares. At the end of each day she writes a few sentences about the day in the square. I have another friend who handwrites an average of five pages a night!

Write enough that the important details of special events are included, many insights into your thoughts and feelings are expressed, and enough information is presented to show what makes you tick in a physical, spiritual, and emotional sense.

Keep in mind that when and how much you write don't really matter as long as you are doing something and growing from the experience. Remember, something, *anything*, is better than nothing.

Types of Journals

There are no right or wrong ways in how you decide to keep a journal. I go through phases of different styles all the time. Louise Plummer, in her book *Thoughts of a Grasshopper* (Salt Lake City: Deseret Book, 1990), has a great chapter titled "The Five-Minutes-a-Day Journal." She describes setting a timer for five minutes and "rush writing" for that time: Write as fast as you can, never allowing your pen to leave the paper. The advantage of this is that you write your thoughts before you can censor them, worrying that they are stupid or that you are spelling something wrong.

Plummer also talks about writing your dreams, poems, reflections on life, lists, and free writing. In free writing you write down whatever comes to your head. Sometimes it makes sense, but other times it is just a lot of unconnected thoughts and feelings.

Lists could include serious things, such as all your blessings, or funny things, such as everything that is in your wallet or on top of your dresser right now. These lists sound silly, but they can be very enlightening.

"Unsent letters" is an area that I love the most. These are not the frustrated, cathartic type of letters (although they end up being cathartic anyway) but rather letters you would like a person to read if he or she could. For example, you might write a letter to a loved one who has died or a thank-you note to an author whose book you have just enjoyed.

It doesn't matter if your journal is fact-and-feeling writing, poetry, dialogue, or drawings. Do what best describes you and your life at that time.

Hints

Write the date. Okay, this might seem obvious, but you'd be surprised how easy it is to forget. I have old writings that carry the day and the month but not the year! (I'm not alone; a lot of people have confessed to this.) I think the day of the week is a good idea too. It might even be fun to write the time of day, the weather conditions, and where you are while writing.

Use last names. Unless you are writing about someone who is absolutely, positively identifiable to another reader, use people's last names! In my life it seems there are an abundance of Daves. Once I was reading back in my own journal from six months earlier. Even *I* didn't know which Dave the entry was about! Now, if I didn't know, surely another reader would never know. I met a girl who told me that her great-great-grandmother ironed shirts for Abraham Lincoln. The only way that the family knows this is from the ancestor's journal, in which she mentioned his full name. They never would have done the research and found out all the facts if she had just written "Abraham" or "Mr. Lincoln."

Include a running table of contents. Update it regularly. You might remember that you had a spiritual experience sometime in the summer, for instance, but it may take you quite a while to find it. But if you had an entry on a contents page: "Spiritual experience, August 2, 1994," you could turn right to it. With a table of contents, important events or feelings for others won't be lost in the year. Topics you might include are feelings for family and friends, spiritual experiences and insights, births, and sad or humorous experiences.

Consider using a three-ring binder instead of a bound journal. Use what works well for you, but here are some reasons why I like a binder. First, I can make sure that I use good, acid-free paper. I also like to type my journal, and a bound book is extremely tough to feed into the typewriter or computer printer! I like to keep a few sheets of journal paper with me so that I can write thoughts and feelings at school, work, or in a waiting room. Many of my entries start out with the words, "I'm sitting here waiting for . . ." Also, I don't have to take my whole journal when I go camping or on a trip. I have heard countless horror stories about people leaving journals on airplanes, in hotels, and so on. Losing a few pages on a trip wouldn't be nearly as devastating as losing a whole volume.

Also, I like to insert things in my journal: invitations, cards, notes, tickets, programs, or articles that pertain to that day. If someone leaves me a kind note, I might as well put it in my journal rather than just write about it there. Keeping these things in a bound journal would eventually break the binding.

Get a journal or notebook you like. I have a binder that has fabric on it that I just love. It makes me feel good just to look at it, and I enjoy writing in it. Some people are intimidated by fancy-looking, formal binders and prefer simple notebooks. Whatever you choose to write in is fine—just make sure that the paper is good quality.

If you type your journal, try to handwrite an entry once

in a while. It's fun to see how our handwriting has evolved over the years. Personality is more evident in our handwriting than in our typing. I think that handwritten materials are more valuable, too. I would much rather have a letter that my grandpa hand-wrote than one that he typed.

Set a regular time to write. This way, it will soon become habitual and a lot easier to do. One woman told me that she just couldn't find the time to write in her journal. I asked her what she did right before she went to bed at night; she answered that she liked to watch the evening news. I challenged her to watch the news with her journal in hand and to write during the commercials. She hasn't missed a day of writing in over a year!

Many people complain about not having enough time to keep a journal. My comeback to this is always, "Well, if President Kimball had time to write thirty-three volumes of journals before he was called as prophet and many more after, we ought to have time!" Consider this: If you think you're too busy to write in your journal, you must be doing some exciting and worthwhile things during your day. Don't you think you should make the effort to record these things? Later in life you might enjoy reading about all the things that kept you so busy!

Don't worry that you're "not a good writer." Schooling makes us obsessed with the mistakes we make in writing. Don't panic if it's not perfect—no one is grading your journal. Your eighth-grade English teacher will never see it. Just put down what is in your mind. Go ahead and cross things out or have run-on sentences. The more you write, the better your skills will become. Write it now; edit it later, if you want. But you can't edit something you haven't written.

Never destroy old journals. One night a woman told me about her past life and how "wild" she was during her high school and college days. Interestingly enough, she kept a journal through the whole period. Now she has changed her ways and is living a clean, straight life. She wondered about her past life and what influence it might have on future generations. Should she burn her journal? The thought struck me so clearly that her journal would be a blessing to her posterity. I was impressed to tell her how thankful I was for the story of the "rotten," prere-pentance life of Alma the Younger in the Book of Mormon. He is my hero, an example of the reality of change, repentance, for-giveness, and the purpose of the Atonement in our lives. But if we didn't have the parts in the Book of Mormon that told how he was wicked and how he repented, we wouldn't appreciate him in quite the same way. The key to all of this, I told her, was to make sure that she was keeping a journal now, while she was living a good life. It wouldn't be as good to have *only* the bad part or even just the good part of Alma the Younger's life. It's the combination that teaches us that when we sin we can be forgiven and live in a way that is pleasing to our Heavenly Father. Her posterity will be able to learn a lot from her life.

I have often told people that it's a good idea to go back to past journals and make a note or two. For example, a woman who wrote a lot about how much she loved one particular boyfriend felt nervous about having anyone read that, since she didn't end up marrying him. She went back to her journal and made a current note (with a date) saying, "Wow, I thought I knew what love was, but since I met [my husband] my thoughts and feelings have changed and matured."

A Child's Journal

My children's journals started out simply as a list of dates of when I took photos. After my first child was born, I would get my pictures back and wouldn't be able to remember the date I took the photos. So, whenever I took a picture, I would jot down something like this: "November 30, 1990, photo of Ceciley on the porch swing in her pink overalls." I then started writing down other important events: "July 5, 1990, laughed out loud," or "June 20, 1991, followed instructions: went and got her sandal and brought it to me." I started writing observations and cute things that she would say and do. Now that she is six, she will tell me things that she wants me to help her write in her journal.

I hope we are establishing habits now that will help her be a good journal writer herself someday.

Another simple way to keep a child's journal is to include it in your own. Just have a section in the back for each child. Each day, as you record in your journal, simply turn to the children's sections and write a little bit about their day, too.

I have created a sample list of children's memorable "firsts" that I like to record:

Raised head alone
Slept all night
Rolled over
Smiled
Laughed
Recognized parents
Discovered hands
Discovered feet
Reached for objects
Sat up alone
Cut a tooth
Held a cup
Crawled
Spoke first word
Had first haircut
Stood up alone
Walked with help
Walked alone

Every month during a child's first couple of years I like to summarize his or her progress. It's fun to look back at the words they spoke, their favorite toys, and funny things that they did during that time of their life. After the child is about two years old, I do a summary twice a year. As soon as the children can draw, I like to add self-portraits.

Every six months or year it's fun to photocopy your children's hands and feet. This is much easier than trying to make copies with ink, and they look great. Experiment with the light and dark settings on the machine. With a good copy you can even see fingerprints. Have the children close or cover their eyes; the light is bright.

Until children can write, have them draw pictures of daily activities or events they want to remember. Then you be the scribe and write what they say about their pictures. This lets them see their own contribution to their journal, and they will be more supportive of the idea of keeping one. As soon as they can write, encourage them to do so along with their drawing. A journal can be a great educational tool.

Asking children questions about an event, and then recording their answers, makes for interesting journal entries. A good question-and-answer session can be generated by having them describe what is happening in a photograph. Dialogues often express the emotion better than a simple description of what children say. Spell the words as they pronounce them (for example, "fick-its" means "fix it" to my son).

Some schoolwork can be added to a journal as well. Many people like to have a separate book for this or add it to a scrapbook. As always, do what works best for you.

Some families have the tradition of presenting children with their first journals (to write in themselves) on their eighth birthdays. The baptism experience is then written about first.

It's important to stress to children that journals show progress. Never let a ten-year-old rip out pages she wrote when she was six. My niece did this because she was embarrassed by her "childish" writing, and she really regrets it now that she is older.

As with any other kind of record keeping, it's useful to set aside a specific time for children to write in their journals. This will lead to good habits for teenagers and adults.

A child's journal is a wonderful way for an adult to relive childhood experiences. I wish that I had anecdotes, dreams, thoughts, and ideas recorded from my childhood. Do whatever you can to encourage children to start keeping a journal. Of course, I feel that keeping one yourself is the best example and motivation you can give.

You're Worth It!

I often hear people say, "Oh, my life isn't very eventful; nobody would be interested." This simply is not true. President Kimball said, "I promise you that if you will keep your journals and records, they will indeed be a source of great inspiration to you, each other, your children, your grandchildren, and others throughout the generations" (*Ensign,* January 1983, p. 3). What a wonderful blessing! I don't know about you, but I'm excited about the possibility of having "great inspiration" in my life. I'm also excited about providing a source of great inspiration to others. You are unique, and your experiences will be treasured by your posterity. Would you be interested in reading your own mother's account of her "boring" daily life? How about her mother's? Someone *will* find your journal interesting. Most of all, it will make great reading for you someday: I promise!

As soon as I accepted the notion that my life was not perfect, nor would it ever be perfect in mortality, it was a whole lot easier for me to write. I have come to understand that I am doing well if my life is a reflection of my continually *trying* to do well. I think it will be refreshing to my posterity to read and know that they don't have to be perfect so long as they are always trying.

You may think that all of the significant or interesting things in your life happened in the past, and that *someday* you will sit down and write them. The present turns into the past quickly, and the past turns into the far past where details can't be recalled. Besides, you will be surprised how interesting the *present* really is. *Start today!* Today make a memory; tonight write it down!

PERSONAL HISTORIES

"You will never turn your own children's hearts more to you than you will if you write a personal history of your life."

HARTMAN RECTOR JR.

Often I am asked, "What is the difference between a history and a journal? If I have one, why do I need the other?" To me, a journal is a day-to-day chronicle of everyday things. My history is a more concise, condensed account of my life. I have volumes and volumes of journals. My personal history is just the highlights, comprising far less writing.

Of all the eight areas of personal record keeping, this is the one that I love the most. When I speak to groups, I like to ask people if they enjoy writing their personal histories. I usually get answers like: "How boring!" or "I will when I'm eighty-five years old," or "My life? No one will care. What should I say?" or "When will I find the time?" If one of those answers could have come from you, I hope that by the end of this chapter you will feel differently about personal histories. There are so many fun and interesting ways to do them.

Why Write a History?

When the Church was first organized, the Prophet Joseph Smith counseled the members to keep a history of the experiences they had, the decisions they made, and the things they

45

learned. I am the beneficiary of such histories from ancestors who knew him personally and followed his counsel. My testimony has grown from reading their experiences. Some of my ancestors, however, did not keep any kind of history. All I know about them is their names and vital dates. Oh, how I wish I knew something—anything—about them! What were their feelings about life? Do we share anything in common?

Knowing our heritage and our ancestors can help us today. An example of this is a friend of mine who was looking for a roommate. She happened upon a girl whose last name was the same as my friend's mother's maiden name. In talking to the girl, my friend found out that they were not-too-distant cousins. My friend had read histories about her cousin's grandfather and they had a lot to talk about. To summarize, they are now happy roommates.

I want to leave my descendants more than just vital statistics. I want them to know who I was and what things, places, and people were important to me. I want to leave a part of me that will go on living after I am not. I want my testimony to help strengthen my family for generations to come.

William Hartley wrote: "Your life thus far has cost nature, your family and many other people a tremendous price in resources, time, effort, and actual dollars expended just to make you become a healthy, capable human being. Is it really asking too much to expect you to leave some accounting of your life, some record of your role in your family, towns, and society? That you give a little credit to those who helped shape you? That you pass along insights and lessons you have learned to the next generation?" (*Preparing a Personal History* [Salt Lake City: Primer Publications, 1976], p. 5.)

Not knowing where and how to begin is probably the biggest obstacle to keeping a personal history. There are many ways to do this, and none of them are necessarily right or wrong. (Well, okay, there is a wrong way. That is to do nothing at all!) The title "Personal History" implies that this record will be kept how you personally want it, not how I say it should be done. You are not writing "Anita's History." Each history should reflect the personality of the person writing it. Only you can decide how to do it.

This chapter will share some ways to write a history that are unique and fun, as well as some that are more traditional. Choose one (or more) that fit your style. Or, better yet, make up your own way!

Chronological Histories

Probably the most common way of writing a personal history is to do it chronologically. Start from as far back as you can remember and recall events from your childhood up to now. Before you begin writing, though, consider these suggestions that might make the process easier.

Brainstorm. Your brain is an incredible organ. It contains a record of everything you have ever done, seen, heard, felt, or experienced. Nothing has been erased from your brain. Through hypnosis people can be brought back to remember even the day they were born. Much of your available recall, however, is selective. Although you may think you have forgotten many things, it's possible to "jog your memory," exercise those brain cells, and remember. This process is called *brainstorming*. Here's how it is done:

Take one topic, event, or idea to reflect on. Try to remember absolutely everything you can about it. Little details lead to other events and details. I do my best brainstorming right before I fall asleep. I lie in my bed and ponder about what it is I am trying to remember. (I've learned that I have to keep a pad of paper by the bed to write notes; otherwise, I've forgotten again by the next day.)

It's also helpful to brainstorm with family and friends. Everybody remembers different things, and one story "feeds" upon another. When you put everyone's details together, it is amazing what you can come up with. Remember to take notes!

Ask others. I'm the youngest child of seven. I've found that one of the best ways for me to recall my early years and events from my past has simply been to ask others about them. My parents and older brothers and sister remember more of my early years than I do. Friends and neighbors have also shared anecdotes that have aided me in putting together my early years.

View the past. Viewing the past can also help you remember things. When I see an old doll or toy, I recall times that I played with them. Seeing my old kindergarten schoolroom recently brought back a flood of memories. When the home that I lived in for my first four years went up for sale, my mother, a brother, and I went to the open house. I was amazed at how many memories I recalled by walking through the home and the yard.

Reading old diaries and journals can help too, as well as looking at old photos, schoolwork, or letters. Any item from the past can help jog your memory of these times and allow you to recall and write about them.

Outline. Topics, life events, or dates are good entries with which to start an outline of your life. List on a sheet of paper the major events of your life along with corresponding dates. Or you can flip-flop the idea and write down dates as the major headings, then write topics or events you can remember that fit into those years. Either way, once you have them written down, you can begin putting together a basic outline. After creating the outline, you can expand upon the topics or significant events one at a time, including subcategories if you wish. Then, after you have written about several topics, you can tie them together in a history.

I was challenged to complete my personal history by a friend who said that she didn't have time to write hers. I took the challenge and made an event outline in about three to five minutes. I then sat down and turned on the timer for fifteen minutes. I typed a basic outline of my life easily in that time. I kept that rough draft on my dresser for a month, during which time I would go back and write things in the margins that I had left out. For example, my grandmother lived with our family for seven years. This was a big part of my life, but somehow I had left it out of my original outline, so I wrote her name in the margin.

Then a month later I took another ten minutes and retyped the history with the additions. I then had a fairly complete, basic outline of my life that has been easy to expand upon.

Use index cards or folders. Another way to start a chronological history is to do it the way our English teachers had us do research papers. Begin by identifying one event or story on an index card. When you have compiled quite a few cards, start filing them chronologically (or in categories, if you prefer). In this way, you can write about events as they come to your mind without worrying about their order, and then you can organize them chronologically later. Once you feel that you have written a card about everything that you want to include, you can write your history from your cards.

I've had many people tell me that they always thought they would write their life history sometime in their eighties. By then you may have forgotten what you meant to write! However, if you have been keeping cards throughout your life, it won't be hard at all.

A variation on the index-card method is to use manila folders to divide up your life into sections. Each folder could have a specific subject such as preschool, elementary school, middle school, high school, adulthood, marriage, and so on. Stories and information can be written on single sheets and then organized in the sections.

Answer questions. In Chapter 5 of this book, "Family Histories," there is a list of questions you might ask when interviewing a family member. Try answering them for yourself, too. The compilation of the questions and answers makes a great history.

A video or audio tape that has you answering questions will be a cherished treasure. Read Chapter 10, "Audio and Video Histories," for hints on how to proceed.

Turn to calendars and day planners. A detailed day planner or calendar is a great help when writing your history. I have referred to mine many times when looking for dates, recalling events, or putting things in chronological order. The more detailed your calender, the better the history. Please, however, don't rely on these to be your sole history. People usually use them to record events but rarely to record feelings.

Categorical Histories

My favorite way to do a personal history is according to categories, groupings, or life periods. I promise you that if you organize a book in this way, it will be your favorite, most priceless book. It will become an addicting activity as well—you will love it!

What I have done is to take a regular three-ring binder and divide it into sections. Whenever I think of an event or story that would fit into a particular category or section, I write it down there. (Okay, what I often do is write a reminder about it on a "sticky note" and stick it in the section. Then, when I have several notes, I write them up all at once.) Sometimes I photocopy an entry out of my journal. Some of the things I include are one-liners, others are lists, and some entries are written by others people.

Following are the different sections that I have used:

> First-time events
> Embarrassing or humorous experiences
> Vacations
> Trials and sad times
> Traditional family stories
> Significant places
> People who have influenced me
> Pets
> Cars
> Friends
> Things I wish I had done, or done differently
> I nearly died when . . .
> Family traditions
> Holiday traditions
> Spiritual experiences

Attitudes and beliefs on life
Circumstances when I was born
Family occupations
Hobbies and talents
Sicknesses
Homes and neighborhoods I've lived in
I'm so glad I . . .
Books I've read
Church callings
Times of joy
Jobs
Hopes, dreams, and fears
Things I love
Frustrations
Relationships and experiences with parents
Brothers and sisters
Dating experiences
If I hadn't . . . , then . . .

Obviously, this list is not all-inclusive. You can have whatever sections you want, but this and the following explanations might give you a start and help you think of topics pertinent to you.

First-time events. This section includes stories about our old Oldsmobile Cutlass convertible, the first car I ever drove. I've written about the first time I went to Yellowstone and Lake Powell, my first airplane ride, my first date, the first pie I baked, my first time to Disneyland, first time to the temple, and so on.

Embarrassing and humorous experiences. This is one of my biggest sections, and that fact is a little embarrassing in itself. It includes stories about getting locked in at a state park, asking the dairyman on a school field trip which color of cows gave the chocolate milk, and tripping in front of a thousand people at a national sorority convention while accepting an award. This section is pretty self-explanatory.

Vacations. In this section I write about where and when we went, with whom, and some of the highlights. I usually include a photo or two, but not too many, since I don't want this turning into a scrapbook. I also include ideas for going to that place again. For example, we recently returned from Disneyland. On Friday, the lines were twice as long as they were on Thursday. I made a note that if we go there again we will know to attend early in the week if possible.

Trials and sad times. Believe it or not, this section is heartwarming to read. I have included feelings about the deaths of my father and father-in-law, and stories of some challenging health problems. This is also one of those sections that can bring perspective and show growth.

Significant places. There are some places that have sentimental significance to me. One of those places is a bench right outside the Huntsman Center ticket office at the University of Utah. This is where I met my husband. The University Medical Center is where my children were born. There are some traditional places that my family likes to visit, and I've written about them.

People who have influenced my life. This section is filled with my accolades to so many people. It's fun for me to share a few thoughts about people who have added to my life. My first-grade schoolteacher, for example, is a real hero to me. Because of some things that she said, I have learned to absolutely love books and reading. Now she is a hero not just to me but also to many others—her name is Chieko Okazaki, and she became widely known for her service as first counselor in the general Relief Society presidency. I have to say that she is still teaching me.

Friends. In the chapter on journals, I mentioned that it is a good idea to share the love and feelings you have for family and friends. Well, this is another place where I put those feelings. In fact, if you have described your feelings for friends in your journal, you could photocopy those entries and include them here. When I talk about my friends I like to mention things that we have done together, or ways they have strengthened me.

Things I wish I had done, or done differently. I wish that I had practiced the piano more. I wish I had used fluoride as a child. You get the idea.

Holiday traditions. Here I explain about how I like to prepare all green food on St. Patrick's Day, and orange and black food on Halloween. Christmas and birthday traditions are also described. For example, we have to get dressed, make our beds, and eat the traditional sweet rolls before we can see what Santa put under the tree.

Spiritual experiences. I love to turn to this section when I'm feeling a bit "spiritually down" and read about all the many miracles in my life and prayers that have been answered. It's nice to have a place where I can group all these experiences together. Because I like to write about a spiritual experience in my journal right when it happens, I usually write it there and then photocopy it and put it here too. My testimony is also written here. Testimonies are changeable things. They grow and develop, and sometimes specific aspects become more prominent in our hearts and minds. Because of this, I update my testimony page and put in a new one from time to time—but I always leave the old one there, too. This section is like my own personal scriptures.

Attitudes and beliefs. This section includes very serious beliefs, such as how I feel about abortion, as well as some lighter feelings, such as how I hate litter. It also contains some of my quirky attitudes, like how much I love fallen leaves—I love them on the ground! I don't like them all raked up. Once the Scouts came and did their "good deed" of raking leaves in the neighborhood, including my yard. When I saw what had happened, I was so sad. I caught up with them and they agreed to dump all the neighborhood leaves in my backyard. I loved it, and my good-natured husband put up with it. I wish that I knew more about the attitudes and beliefs that my grandparents carried through their lives.

Family occupations. Whenever I speak to a group, I ask the people to raise their hands if they know what both of their grandfathers did for a living. Usually about half know. Then I ask if any know what all four of their great-grandfathers did. There is

53

sometimes one person who does. What this tells me is that, statistically, only about half of us will have children who know what our father's occupation was. Few of us will have grandchildren who know about our father's occupation. Something so commonplace and basic to us will be lost to future generations if we don't write about it.

Sicknesses. Whenever I have a check-up at the doctor's office, I am asked, "Is there any history of high blood pressure, cancer, diabetes, etc., in your family?" If you do have some health concern that others should know about, write it down. It's also fun to write about average health problems and how they affected you. For example, do you have hay fever? How do you deal with it?

I'm so glad I . . . This is often just a collection of fill-in-the-blank sentences such as "I'm so glad I was born in the family I was." At times I expound a bit. For example: "I'm so glad I joined the sorority in college that I did; because of it I met my husband."

Books. I like to write down the title of the book I just finished, the date, and how I liked it. It's interesting to look back over the years and see what I have read. It also serves others if they ask for reading recommendations.

Church callings. Here I tell what my callings have been, with whom I served, and some of the activities and unique things we did.

Things I love. This is simply a list. Some of them are: cotton candy, hats, dolls, nursing my babies, going out to lunch, roller coasters, root beer, cinnamon candy, jumping with my children on the trampoline, being at the cabin, working on my scrapbooks, slippery slides . . .

Frustrations. This is my newest category. I never have had much problem choosing between right and wrong. However, my biggest frustration is choosing between right and right. For example, some friends and I got rodeo tickets for a certain Friday night. We'd been so excited about this night and had talked and planned for months. I then found out that my niece's last dance concert (which I *really* wanted to attend) was the same night! UGH!

If I hadn't . . . , then . . . If I hadn't been a sorority adviser, then I never would have been able to line up the countless couples that I have. (Names are withheld here to protect the involved, but there are many!) A dear friend of mine once became quite ill and was confined to bed. As she looked out her window onto a vacant lot, she felt it should be turned into a park. While in bed she made the necessary connections to bring that dream to reality. So, her history could say that if she hadn't gotten sick, then that park wouldn't exist. Here's one for you to figure out: If I hadn't contracted a mononucleosis virus, then you'd never be reading this book.

I love my category book. There are many reasons why I feel this is a good way to do a history. One is that events in the past can come back to me at any time. I don't have to fret that my history is already written and that those events won't fit in chronologically. For example, my brother recently reminded me about the first time he took me on a roller coaster. It was a funny story I wanted to remember, so I wrote about it, figured out the year as well as I could, and put it in my "First-time" section.

Another reason I like the categories method is that it tells more about me as an individual than a chronological history might. For example, the contents of a lot of the categories (things I love, for instance) just wouldn't fit anywhere chronologically. Additionally, it wouldn't be too hard for anyone to find out how many brothers and sisters I had, what high school I attended, or what field my college degree was in (things usually included in a chronological history). But, without a categorical history to look at, even a private investigator would have a tough time finding out about my spiritual experiences, my attitudes and beliefs, or things I wish I had done differently.

As you can tell from the headings, some of the category sections are just one-word lists. Some are more detailed. Whatever works for you is just fine. There are no rules here.

Special Event Histories

It's interesting to read about past yearly events on the day of the current event. For example, it's always fun to read on Thanksgiving Day about past Thanksgivings. I have a Thanksgiving book that tells about who came to dinner, who brought what dish, and so on. It includes some photos of the occasion. We have had a fun tradition over the years of a family "weigh-in." Everyone who wants to weighs in before dinner and then again after. Then we see who gained the most weight on a percentage basis. (Sounds like I grew up in a family of boys, doesn't it?) I have kept records of a lot of weigh-ins, and it's fun to go back and look at them.

Any holiday provides a good subject for a history—Christmas, Easter, New Year's Day. They all come once a year and are good times to write feelings. I especially like doing this on my birthday. Each year I write what I call my "Birthday Personal State of the Union." It tells what is happening with me and within my circle of family and friends at that time of my life. It's not usually a very long document; it takes only a few minutes to do. I write about my current Church calling, my favorite food, book, movie, song, TV show, color, dessert, hobby/pastime, store, and so on. I also tell a bit about what is happening in the world. This is another good place to include descriptions of current news items and fads and fashions. I like to record who the president and vice president of the United States are, the minimum wage, and the average prices of bread, milk, homes, and cars for that year. In 1979 I wrote: "This year I have seen gas prices go from 46 cents to 84 cents a gallon and higher! In California the gas lines are miles long. Some say the price will go to a dollar a gallon, but I doubt it!"

A mountain-climbing friend of ours keeps a climbing history. Every time he goes climbing, he records who he went with, what climb they did, and some feelings about it. This could be done with any hobby.

Some people buy score books and keep score at each Little

League game their children play in. My brother has done this for years. He writes a quick summary or highlight after each game. Much of the drama of a sporting event is forgotten over time if not recorded. I would like to have kept a record of my bowling progress the year my husband and I substituted on a bowling league. It was fun seeing my scores rise from a pathetic 30 to over 100.

When these event histories are kept together, they become a quick summary of one's life history. They act as a "reality check" or a measuring stick for growth. They are also often enlightening and funny.

You can see that these topics could also fit nicely into your category book, if you have one. Some of them are nice to have in a binder by themselves. Whatever works best for your system is the right way to do it!

Time Capsules

A time capsule is entertaining for people of all ages, and a great resource for future generations. I'd love to be opening right now a time capsule left behind by a distant ancestor! Paul Hudson, the cofounder of the International Time Capsule Society, says that time capsules reflect a desire to save something for the future. "Our lifetimes are so short, and this is a way that someone a hundred years from now, or even a thousand years from now, can see remnants of our lives. It's that urge for immortality we all have." Hudson talks about the possibility of leaving capsules for a hundred years. I feel it's good to *keep* them that long, but exciting to open them in five or ten years. (Chances are, you won't be here in a hundred years to enjoy them.) You can always seal them back up again if you haven't gone so far as to encase them in concrete.

Things to include in a time capsule could be: newspapers and magazines, children's schoolwork, a paycheck stub, vacation memorabilia, programs, fliers, sport uniforms, photos, collectibles such as stamps, coins, or baseball cards, letters, copies of certificates or records, clothing, receipts, anything you want.

Select a safe container. A dark container that can be sealed tight is best. It is usually a good idea to not include food items, due to their potential for spoilage and attraction to rodents and bugs. Interesting empty food wrappers or containers can be just as good. Avoid burying your time capsule, as it is too easy to lose. Many people have encased capsules in footings of new home additions, decks, or fences. This can be frustrating, especially if your family moves. Although it's not as exciting as burying the capsule, placing it on a shelf in your storage room is probably safer and more likely to be remembered. Make sure the existence and location of a time capsule are prominently recorded for those you want to know of it.

Choose a retrieval date; then don't forget! A holiday or significant date is easiest to remember. Making time capsules a tradition is great fun. One family prepares a capsule every New Year's Eve, then opens an old one on New Year's Day.

Try preparing a capsule that is significant to an event. For example, a wedding capsule could contain your wedding invitation, newspaper article, a piece of cake (if you're careful), garter, handkerchief, photos, a copy of the certificate, lace from the wedding dress, fabric from bridesmaids' dresses, and honeymoon mementoes. This would be of great interest to open on an anniversary or on the eve of your first child's wedding. A similar capsule could be created for a birth, graduation, or any other event.

Have a capsule ceremony. Make a production of having everyone add an item for storage and tell why it is meaningful for him or her. Videotape the ceremony and put the tape in the capsule. Whatever you do, make it fun and memorable.

Write a letter. A sort of "mini" time capsule can be created by simply writing a letter and keeping it sealed for a period of time. As a teenager, I did this at the first of the year for many years. I would write down my dreams and desires for the year and my hopes of what would be happening at the same time next year. Then each year I would open the letter from the past. It's interesting to see how perspectives and thoughts can change over a period of time.

Soliciting the Help of Others

Getting other people involved in helping you write your history is really quite beneficial. When my dad turned sixty-five years old, we presented him a "This Is Your Life" night. Beforehand we went around and taped interviews with his family, friends, and coworkers. We then transcribed the tapes onto paper in book form. I learned so much about my dad that I had never known! The information we gained has been a big asset to his history.

Recently I received a letter, part of which follows (Joe is my husband, Ceciley is my five-year-old daughter):

Dear Joe and Anita,

I just have to tell you about a most pleasant holiday experience I had involving Joe and Ceciley.

About a week before Christmas I was in Shopko, which of course was a madhouse—crowded, long lines, crying, tired children, etc. While waiting in a checkout line and hearing all the crying and scolding around me, I caught sight of a man and child skipping across the front of the store hand in hand. Immediately, my mind changed directions as I thought that at least a few people knew how to have fun at Christmastime.

As they came close enough to where I was standing and waiting, I could see that it was Joe and Ceciley headed for the door!

That was a choice, memorable experience for me that day and one I will long remember. Thanks, Joe, for being such a good, happy father and not falling into the trap that the stress of the holidays all too often brings . . .

Now, I could list my husband's qualities in a personal history. But this letter describes him perfectly! As you can see, the perspective of others and their insights can add a dimension to your history that otherwise would be lost.

We don't often receive letters like this one, so sometimes we simply need to ask for them. This past year I sent a letter to my brothers and sister telling them that all I wanted for my birthday was their remembrances of when I was born. The stories I received were so entertaining and have added a wonderful dimension to my history. My older siblings are much better informed about my early years than I am.

Here is an enlightening activity you can do to obtain responses from others. At a get-together of family or friends, place a pile of appropriate photos on a table. Ask each person to choose one that he or she knows about. After they have chosen their photos, ask them to take ten minutes to write everything they remember about that particular activity or event. When everyone is finished, read them aloud. I was amazed when I did this with some friends. A girlfriend and I chose photos from the same trip. After reading the stories out loud, you would have felt that we were on two totally different vacations! Our perceptions, feelings, and remembrances were so different. Neither of us was wrong; we just saw things differently. It's always good to get another perspective.

News Events

A few important components of your history are news stories, current events, fads, and fashions. For example, I remember watching Neil Armstrong walk on the moon on July 20, 1969. Although I can remember it, I surely wish that I had kept a newspaper or magazine from then. I also wish that I had written about the experience. The years melt away a lot of thoughts and feelings.

Things that happen around us help to make up who we are. We should be consciously aware of events, then clip and include news articles and write about how we feel about them. Barney Clark, the first artificial heart patient, was in a hospital just miles from my home. His surgery was big news. I remember how interesting it was to follow his progress and almost feel a part of the whole experience. I recall how an older neighbor felt that Barney couldn't love anymore without a "real" heart!

The coming down of the Berlin Wall was another event of personal interest to me. My brother was serving a mission there when the wall went up, and his daughter, my niece, was there on a mission when it came down.

All of these events (and more) have had an impact on my life. We should write about our feelings and attitudes concerning what is going on in the world around us.

Fashions and fads are also amusing to write and read about. Clothing styles that we thought were so good looking twenty or thirty years ago seem so funny, odd, and even embarrassing now. I periodically save some ads to show the styles and prices of the times.

The newspaper usually prints a "Top News Items of the Year" page at the end of December. This is a fun article to keep. I also like to pick up a magazine that offers the "Year in Pictures" as well. The articles and pictures are nice to have, but they're even better if you can also write your feelings about the top items of the year.

Television programs, movies, best-selling books, plays, music, and sporting events (World Series and Super Bowl winners) can all be recorded easily now, but will be just as easily forgotten with time. Record what is interesting to you.

You can intermix news items with your chronological history or put them into your category history. Or you could keep a separate book specifically for news items. Articles can also be inserted into a yearly scrapbook very easily.

Newsletters and Letters

Probably one of the best ways I've seen a personal history done is from a newsletter created by my brother's family. For about twenty-five years he and his family have faithfully written a monthly newsletter. Once a month they summarize the previous month. My brother does the first page, and then each family member fills in a page of his or her own. My nieces have been on missions and away at college and are now all married, and they still submit their articles for the "Tannery Times." Once the newsletter is written, it is then copied and mailed to family across the country. This way we all keep up to date on their lives. More importantly, however, each family member has a notebook with the newsletters from the past twenty-five years. What a wonderful history! Even if you don't want to do a newsletter, if once a month you summarized the previous month, your life history would be written.

A variation on the newsletter is our family minutes. Once a month my brothers and sisters and our children who are living in town meet for a family meeting. All kinds of things happen at that meeting, but one good historical thing is that minutes are taken. Each family tells news and events of the past month (or events coming up). These are recorded in the minutes. Over the past twenty years I have turned to my minutes many times for information. I'm very thankful for them.

My mother has used carbon paper in her typewriter for years when she writes a letter to family members. Combining these copies in a notebook gives her a great personal history. With computers and copy machines available it is easier than ever to write letters and keep copies for our own records. A "newsy" letter can be one of the best types of history.

"Circling letters" are good for preserving history about family members or friends. One person starts the letter, then mails it to another, who in turn writes and mails it on to another. This goes on until the letter has gone full circle. This is a good way to get a letter from someone who procrastinates writing. The incentive to write is stronger when you know people are waiting and counting on you!

I like to keep letters and cards that are written to me. They usually include great information worth preserving. I have a folder for each year in which I keep the letters I received that year. Some special notes and letters go into other places, such as my journal and scrapbook, but it's always fun to get out a past folder and read letters I've received.

A Letter to Posterity

Periodically I write letters to my children. These letters are for them to read at a future date. I have a lot of feelings and thoughts about my children and their future. If I didn't write these thoughts while they were on my mind, I would likely forget them. When the children are old enough to understand, they can read the letters and know how I felt at that time of our lives. My hope is that these letters can bring encouragement to them throughout their lives and give them an understanding of their mother's desires and values. This is a type of personal history in and of itself.

During the thirty-nine hours of labor awaiting the birth of my daughter, my husband had some time on his hands. He wrote the most beautiful letter to her (at that time not knowing who she was), expressing many feelings that he had at the time. Those feelings would have been lost had he waited to write the letter until she was old enough to read and understand it.

I want my children to know how I feel about them right now. I know that when my daughter is eighteen years old, I won't remember exactly how I thrilled at her six-year-old ways. There is no better way to keep that memory than to write it right now.

Personal Papers

Personal papers that we don't often think about tell a lot about us. I keep a folder of these items (originals or photocopies), which are interesting for future generations and amusing to me as well. Examples of some things included in the folder are:

A to-do list from a very busy day
Résumés
Job reviews
Loan applications
Paycheck stubs
Interesting receipts
An unusual traffic ticket

63

A bowling score card
New Year's resolutions
Goals

Helpful History Hints

1. Give details. Don't tell only what you did, but *how you felt.* Think about what a person living a hundred years from now would want to know about you and your experiences.

2. Avoid writing as if your history were a graded college research paper. Write as you would talk if you were telling your feelings or the story in person.

3. I love reading words that I used to say, such as *nifty, swell,* and *groovy.* However, be careful when using words or phrases that would cause someone in the future to have no idea what you're talking about. For example, the word *bad* can now at times mean something really "cool" (or is it "hot"?); anyway, it doesn't necessarily mean "rotten," but rather "good."

4. Start! I repeat, there is no right or wrong way to keep a personal history. Your way is the best way for you. Choose one of the ways I have described, mix ideas together, or invent your own way. Just do it! Write whatever comes to your mind. You can always go back and edit later, but you cannot edit or correct something you don't have! Capture as many feelings and events as you can before you forget.

FAMILY HISTORIES

"You're not an accident of birth; someone has paid the price to get you here. These are noble people. Maybe they've never had an opportunity to write [their history] themselves, but you can write it."

HARTMAN RECTOR JR.

Elder Theodore M. Burton wrote: "Much of what we now regard as scripture was not anything more or less than men writing of their own spiritual experiences for the benefit of their posterity. These scriptures are family records. Therefore, as a people we ought to write of our own lives and our own experiences to form a sacred record for our descendants. We must provide for them the same uplifting, faith-promoting strength that the ancient scriptures now give us" (*Ensign,* January 1977, p. 17).

Family histories can bring eternal families closer together. Elder John H. Groberg said: "As we contemplate what those before us have gone through that we might be here, as we sense their faith and courage and feel their love for us and our love for them, we realize what is really important. We begin to comprehend the eternity of the family" (*Ensign,* May 1980, p. 48).

As you can see, family histories are important if not vital to have. But what is a family history? Simply put, a family history is your own and your extended family's personal histories, biographies, and life sketches all put together. It can be organized to include an immediate family, one generation, or several generations. Family histories usually contain the same kinds of information as personal histories. In addition, they may include information about the family's national origin, places of residence, occupations, world and local events that affected the family as a whole, histories of hometowns, conversion stories, and so on.

Writing a family history can be a challenge. Most of us have a hard enough time getting our own personal histories done. Attempting to write about people who have died is difficult, as reliable information can be hard to come by. Motivating other family members to participate in the process can at times cause frustration—until they themselves begin to feel the excitement and value of the work.

Family histories are like personal histories in that there is no set way to do them. The important thing is that *something* be done. This chapter will give ideas to help you get started—use them in any combination or make up your own.

I have found that the best way to get a history from a living family member is to help him or her. For example, one of my friends had tried for years to get her grandmother to write her history. Nothing ever worked. Finally she figured out a subtle way to get the information that she wanted. Her grandmother lived in another state and they corresponded by letter quite a bit. My friend started asking questions in the letters such as "How did you and Grandpa meet?" Each letter contained a pertinent question. The grandma wrote back wonderful letters with each of my friend's questions answered in great detail. (She didn't know she was writing a history; she just thought she was answering a question for her granddaughter!) In about a year's time my friend had a wealth of information and put together a beautiful history of her grandmother.

Another woman gave her mother sheets of paper with a different question on the top of each for her birthday. She then attached a letter saying that what she wanted for Christmas was for her mother to fill in each page and give them back to her.

Interviewing

Interviewing family members is another good way to get histories. Be sure to take accurate notes. Use a tape recorder or video camera if available.

Interviews can be either spontaneous or planned. If Grandpa starts to talk to you about his life during dinner, sometimes it totally halts the conversation to say "Stop! Let me run and get the tape recorder." Just let him talk. Sometimes people are more open in a casual conversation than in a formal interview. Remember as many of the details as possible and jot them down as soon as you can after the interview.

When conducting a planned interview, try not to do so under circumstances that are too formal. If you know beforehand that a particular activity is one where good storytelling conversations take place, schedule an interview for then. Familiar surroundings will help to distract from the fact that people are being interviewed and that possibly a video camera or tape recorder are being used.

Here are some suggestions to help in interviewing.

1. In a planned interview, give the person being interviewed a list of some questions you will be asking beforehand. This allows the person to start pondering answers and will make for a better interview.

2. If a recorder is being used, say the complete names, date, and place of the interview on the tape at the beginning and at the end of your interview.

3. Avoid asking questions that have yes-or-no answers. There is nothing inherently wrong with these questions except that they aren't very interesting.

4. Find out as much as you can about the person before your interview. This makes your questions more pertinent and can avoid a possibly embarrassing situation.

5. Show interest. Nothing can kill an interview faster than an interviewer who looks bored! Interject remarks whenever

appropriate, making sure to not dominate the conversation. Be a good listener as well as a good questioner. Keep it fun and relaxed.

6. Be prepared with a list of questions to ask, but don't be afraid to let your interviewee go off on a tangent. The person might end up talking about a subject that becomes more interesting and insightful than your list of prepared questions.

7. Never stop taking notes or turn off a recorder until you are *sure* the person is finished, unless asked to. This can suggest to the interviewee that you think the information is not worth writing or recording. Have a pen and paper with you even if you are recording on tape. This way you can write a note when you think of a question, instead of interrupting to ask it.

8. Use props if at all possible. Documents, letters, photo albums, family heirlooms, artifacts, and quilts are just some of the things that can be used to stimulate memories and conversation.

9. Don't be afraid of a little silence. Allow the interviewee time to ponder. Sometimes silence is necessary for gathering thoughts.

10. Be sensitive to the individual's needs. Schedule your planned sessions at convenient times. Older people (and younger, for that matter) sometimes tire easily. Stop the interview at the first sign of fatigue and schedule another time to finish. One-hour segments work best.

11. Make sure that you give a transcript of your interview to all involved. Save all your notes, tapes, and documentation. Label them all with the date, place, names of interviewee and interviewer, ages, and relationship.

12. Respect confidences and privacy.

13. Do it now before it may be too late.

14. Once your history is transcribed on paper, send a copy to a local library or historical society. Someday a distant cousin may find it there and be grateful for your work.

15. If taping with audio or video cassettes, please see Chapter 10, "Audio and Video Recordings," for additional hints on recording most effectively.

Questions and Topics for Interviews

The following topics suggest good questions to ask yourself for your own personal history as well as for interviewing others for family histories. The topics in the category section of Chapter 4, "Personal Histories," are also good for stimulating conversations during interviews. Remember that these questions are meant to be suggestions, not an absolute format. Pick and choose among them as you see fit. The most useful questions will be those that you develop through your knowledge of yourself and your family. By all means, change words and phrases to suit your own personality and situation.

1. **Vital statistics.** Tell dates and any interesting stories surrounding your birthday, birthplace, blessing, baptism, confirmation, any other ordinance dates, marriage date, and education—places and degrees.

2. **Family.** Describe your father, mother, and brothers and sisters. Tell of their personalities, stature, temperament, talents, careers, and interests. What are some fun or significant stories about them? If possible, tell about your cousins, aunts, uncles, and grandparents.

3. **Early childhood.** What toys, games, and hobbies did you like as a child? What homes did you live in? What are some memories of home? Describe your yard, your bedroom, any other rooms you remember. What were the neighborhoods like where you lived? Tell about your neighbors. Were any of them famous? Did you have any household chores as a child? What friends did you have as a child? What kinds of things did you do or play? Were there any sad times or special experiences you remember from your childhood? Did you cause your parents trouble? How did they handle it? Describe birthday parties you remember. What were your favorite clothes? What childhood illnesses did you have? Do you remember any little poems or songs from your childhood?

4. **School years.** What elementary, junior high, and high schools did you attend? Tell about some teachers you remember.

What were your favorite subjects? Did you participate in any extracurricular activities? What activities did you attend? Who were your friends? What special family activities do you remember during those times? What interests or hobbies did you have? What experiences did you have getting your driver's license and driving a car?

5. **Home remedies.** Describe any home cures for hiccups, warts, toothaches, colds, earaches, flu, fever, and so on.

6. **Jobs, vocations, career.** What was your first job? What were your duties? How much did you earn? What subsequent jobs have you had? Describe your current or most recent job and career. Who were some of the people you worked with? What were your parents' careers? What were the economic conditions of your family growing up? If you could do it all over again, would you choose the same career? Do you have any advice on the subject?

7. **Favorites.** What is your favorite flower, color, place, store, restaurant, season . . . ?

8. **Church.** Can you remember going to church as a child? What were some of your feelings about God? What memories do you have of Scouts, Mutual, Primary? Who were your leaders? What lessons or activities stand out in your mind? What were some of the things that increased your testimony of the gospel? What Church callings have you had? Whom did you serve with? What Church callings did your parents have? Tell some of your favorite scriptures and why they are important to you. Did you serve a mission? Tell about your companions and experiences.

9. **Sports.** What sports have you enjoyed participating in or watching? If you played, what position(s) did you play? How skilled were you? What teams did you play on and which did you root for?

10. **Pets.** Tell of any pets you have had in your life. What were their names? What funny quirks did they have? What other animals do you like?

11. **Music.** What types of music do you like? Do you have any memories associated with music? Have you ever played a

musical instrument? Did you play in a band or orchestra, or sing in a choir?

12. **College.** Did you attend a college or university? What degree did you earn? What extracurricular activities did you participate in? Did you study abroad?

13. **Military.** Did you serve in the military? Where were you stationed? What ranks did you earn? Did you receive any commendations? Did you serve in combat? Describe your feelings about your service.

14. **Dating.** Who was the subject of your first crush? Tell about early romances in your life.

15. **Marriage.** How did you meet your spouse? How did you first meet your in-laws? When, where, and to whom were you married? Describe your wedding day, honeymoon, first home, and first years of married life.

16. **Married family life.** How many children did you have? Where and when were they born? What were some of the special things you did with your children? What are some projects you worked on together as a family? What are some things you did to teach your family the gospel? Are there any special or faith-promoting experiences you might relate about your family life? What vacations did you take?

17. **Child rearing.** Tell about your parents' philosophy of child rearing. How is it alike or different from yours?

18. **Accomplishments.** What do you think are your greatest accomplishments? Why do you feel that way? Do you have some lesser but still significant accomplishments?

19. **Media facts.** Who or what are your favorite authors, books, movies, movie stars, professional athletes, heroes, television programs, and radio shows?

20. **Dreams, fears, and other feelings.** What are your dreams? Describe your fears; tell how you dealt with or overcame them. Tell about embarrassing moments.

21. **Community activities.** Have you been involved with any community or service activities? Volunteer work? PTA? What about political interests and involvement?

22. **Personality traits.** What personality traits do you admire? What traits have you tried to incorporate into your life? What do you value most?

23. **Family names.** What do you know about your family surname (its origin and meaning)? Did it undergo any changes through the years? Are there any traditional first names, middle names, or nicknames in your family? Is there a naming tradition, such as always giving the firstborn son the name of his paternal grandfather?

24. **Traditions.** What traditions have been handed down in your family? Can you sort out the traditions in your current family according to the branches of the larger family from which they have come? Does the overall tradition of a specific grandparent seem to be dominant? Are there any talents or interests that have been handed down, such as quilting, whittling, canning, pottery . . . ?

25. **Family routines.** Describe your daily family routine. Did your family gather together for meals, scripture reading, prayers, or family councils? What was mealtime like? Did Dad or Mom leave for work early? Was it an ordeal to get children ready for bed or school?

26. **Hobbies.** What have been your favorite hobbies, activities, and talents?

27. **"Black sheep."** Do you have a notorious or infamous character in your family's past?

28. **Love stories.** How did your parents, grandparents, and other relatives come to meet and marry? Are there family stories of lost love, jilted brides, unusual courtships, arranged marriages, elopements, runaway lovers?

29. **The world outside.** How have historical events affected your family? For example, how did your family survive the Depression? What about wars or natural disasters?

30. **Family finance.** Are there any family stories of how a great fortune was lost or made? Was your family frugal or extravagant regarding family finances? Did you receive or give allowances? How much? How did you learn the value of money?

31. **Family vocabulary.** What verbal expressions or sayings are used in your family? Did they come from specific incidents? Are there stories that explain their origin? Is a particular member of the family especially adept at creating expressions?

32. **Holidays.** How are holidays such as Christmas, Easter, New Year's, Thanksgiving, and Halloween celebrated in your family? What innovations has your family made in holiday celebrations? Has your family created entirely new holiday traditions? Are there some traditional decorations you remember well?

33. **Vacations.** Where have you traveled? What states and countries have you visited? What has been the most exciting or adventurous thing you have done?

34. **Recipes.** Have any recipes been preserved in your family from past generations? Are there traditional foods, customs, or food-related activities? What are your favorite and least favorite foods?

35. **Outside influence.** Are there important people who have influenced your family in some way? Do they participate in your family activities?

36. **Dying.** Is there a family cemetery or burial plot? Who is buried there? How did your family members die?

37. **Heirlooms.** Does your family have any heirlooms— objects of sentimental or monetary value that have been handed down? What are they? Are there stories connected with them? Do you know their origins and lines of passage through the generations?

38. **Turning points.** Have there been any major turning points in your life or in the life of your family?

39. **Spiritual experiences.** Are there any spiritual or faith-promoting experiences that can be shared?

40. **Highs and lows.** What have been your greatest joys and sorrows? What has been your most trying experience? What has been the most wonderful thing that has happened to you? The worst?

41. **Science and technology.** What significant changes have

you seen in your lifetime regarding technological advances? What great inventions have you seen come about?

42. **Closing remarks.** What message would you like to leave your descendants?

Family Recipes

One of my grandmothers, my father's mother, lived in our home for seven years. She made the best homemade rolls ever! She didn't have a recipe written down; she just made them from memory. I have really felt bad that I never paid close attention and took notes while she was making them. No one in the family seems to be quite able to duplicate them.

My other grandmother came from Germany. She had an old stoneware crock in which she made the absolute best sauerkraut in the whole world. I have never been able to find any sauerkraut that comes remotely close to her delicious homemade kraut. Oh, how I wish someone had her recipe!

Many of our childhood memories revolve around food. I'm sure you can think of a food that reminds you of a family member or a particular family event. My husband's family has a tradition of having a special pudding at Christmastime. Granny O (my husband's maternal grandmother) always makes the special sauce, and she makes at least five times what most people would, and yes, it all disappears! Cinnamon sweet rolls are a tradition at our breakfast table on Christmas. My mom's turkey dressing is incredible. (I have written that one down!) These recipes and food memories should be preserved. They are an integral part of any family history.

At the very least, recipes should be copied down on recipe cards or paper. Always write the name of the person who originated the recipe. Was it one he or she invented or just used a lot? Make copies for other family members.

A fantastic thing to do is to compile a family cookbook. You can do this on your own by collecting and compiling recipes, typing them up, and making photocopies.

An alternative is to have a publisher do it for you. Cookbook

Publishers, Inc., is one that I am familiar with. They supply recipe forms, and all you have to do is furnish the recipes. They will compile your personalized book for you. For more information, check the appendix at the end of this book.

Family Newsletters

A family newsletter is just like the newsletter described in the preceding chapter on personal histories, but it involves members of the extended family as contributors. In an extended family newsletter, many families would contribute news items. Perhaps each family could write one page. This need not be done too often; even once or twice a year is good.

Extended family newsletters are great vehicles for sharing stories or histories of ancestors, acknowledging birthdays and special events, or swapping recipes. They can also be a good place to inquire for or supply genealogical information.

Create a Book

One of my favorite pieces of family history is a book that my family affectionately calls the "Spencer Book." I never knew my great-grandfather, Samuel Spencer, but I remember well his fourth wife, whom we called Aunt Lottie. My great-grandfather was born in the Salt Lake Valley only sixteen years after the first pioneers arrived. His father, Daniel Spencer, was the leader of the first company of pioneers that came after Brigham Young. Daniel became the stake president in the Salt Lake Stake of Zion in February 1849. He knew Joseph Smith well, and he and his family were among the Saints driven from place to place in the early years of the Church.

My great-grandfather Samuel inherited many historic newspaper articles, histories, and photographs from his father. Toward the end of her life, Aunt Lottie wondered what would happen to all of these artifacts. How could these priceless things be shared among thirty-eight grandchildren? She determined that it would be much better to keep them together instead of sending fragments of history here and there.

Aunt Lottie had a wonderful vision of making copies for everyone so that all the descendants could share these priceless histories, photos, and articles. My mother spent hours and hours organizing and putting together pages for a beautiful book according to Aunt Lottie's desires. A family reunion was held and individual photos of my great-grandfather's children's families were taken and added to the book.

Producing the books was a huge task in the sixties, when copy machines were not readily available. At a printing shop, enough books were made for everyone, including great-grandchildren.

I have thrilled over the years when, as I study the history of the Church, I can read along in my "Spencer Book" about my own ancestors and their experiences that correlate so well with any other Church history story. I'm thankful to my Aunt Lottie for spending our inheritance in such a meaningful way.

Writing Histories for Others

Obtaining histories directly from some of our relatives may be impossible due to their health problems, memory loss, or physical impairment. Or perhaps they've passed away. Every life is still worth having something written about it. With a little detective work, you can compile a pretty good history of someone's life without that person's help. There are many sources of information that can help you piece together a history.

The first time any of your ancestors set foot in America, someone was writing down their names. No matter how they arrived, by boat or plane, there's a record of it somewhere. If they were born, married, divorced, had children, served in the military, or died, there is a record of it. If they ever applied for citizenship, a passport, or a social security number; if they owned land, attended school, or voted, there was a form filled out. The original or a copy of that form is in an office somewhere. The information on these records can help you find out a lot about your family; licenses and forms often carry the names of the individual's parents as well as important dates.

The following is a list of sources of information that are especially useful. Addresses for many of the sources are listed in the appendix.

1. **Vital records.** These include birth, death, and marriage licenses and certificates.

2. **Other living relatives.** Many family members can give great details about the life of an ancestor. Be sure to verify dates and spelling of names as well as you can. At times different family members will give contradicting dates or other facts. In such cases you will have to evaluate and find more information to determine which version is correct. Record your sources. It's important to know where you got your information. If you don't have proof for a story or information, you cannot claim it as fact.

3. Search **phone books** for possible relatives from different branches of your family that you don't know about.

4. **Close friends and associates of the individual.** These people hold a wealth of knowledge that is great for any history.

5. **Photos, slides, movies, scrapbooks.** These are very valuable in recalling memories and supplying information. You may need others to look with you who can help identify events, names, and feelings.

6. **Diaries and journals.** If you can acquire these from the person you are writing about, you have wonderful, firsthand information. These are probably the most accurate form of information you could find.

7. **Letters.** These share a lot of insight into a person's life. They can also give valuable dates and events.

8. **Wills, probate, tax, insurance, and social security records.** These can also add accurate dates and places. Probate records are usually filed at county courthouses.

9. **Deeds, real estate or land records,** and records of other transactions.

10. **County courthouses.** Write to the county courthouse where an event took place for records of dates.

11. **Cemetery gravestones and cemetery records.** This is a good place for dates and names. Sometimes you can also find an

epitaph that tells a little about the person. Remember that gravestone dates are secondhand information given at a time of grief, and they are hard to correct if a mistake is made. Always check the manager's or office records, not just the gravestones. Some graves have no headstones.

12. **Published genealogies and works from historical societies** and genealogy organizations.

13. **Census records.** In the United States, every ten years since 1790 a census (or head count) has been taken. (The census of 1890, however, was for the most part lost in a fire.) Census takers didn't just count people; they collected a lot of information, including addresses and children's names, ages, and birthplaces. Other census records include veterans of the Civil War.

14. **Church records.** This is a perfect place to find names and dates. Many churches and synagogues kept (and still keep) dates of birth, christenings, and blessings, baptisms, marriages, and deaths.

15. **The Chamber of Commerce and Bureau of Vital Statistics** in the relevant area might have information on your ancestors, particularly if they were involved in civic activities.

16. **Printed material.** School yearbooks, autograph books, city directories, magazines, or printed materials from the community can help recall events.

17. **Newspapers.** These have obituaries as well as birth and wedding announcements. You can usually make a search of newspapers on microfilm or computer at the library.

18. **Immigrant passenger lists, passports, and citizenship documents.** Immigrants were asked a host of questions at the immigration center. These included such information as nationality, occupation, marital status, and literacy.

19. **Family Bibles.** Many important dates and names are placed here. If the dates and names are written in the same handwriting and ink, they could be a summary rather than an ongoing original record. One way to check if they are copied is to see if the dates written in the Bible are earlier than the publication date of that edition. The more accurate Bibles are ones that were

kept as a running record and handed down from one generation to the next. The dates and names were written as they occurred, rather than copied from one source to another.

20. **Community organizations and school records.** Many city and state offices have membership records and minutes.

21. **Obituaries and funeral programs.** These have dates and names.

22. **Birth and wedding announcements and invitations** are another source for names and dates.

23. **Military records.** These often include physical descriptions.

24. **Newsletters.** Find out if the area where your ancestors lived has historical and genealogical organizations. If so, you can subscribe to their newsletters. One woman read a published letter written by her third great-grandfather. It was the clue she needed to make the necessary research to tie into other lines.

25. **State archives and libraries.** Each state has an archive or a state library. (Some have both.) State and county government records are kept there, as well as some federal records, such as U.S. census schedules for the state.

26. **Public and university libraries.** These have many published sources.

27. **Trophies, medals, pins, plaques, and other awards.**

28. **Charts or family trees.**

29. **Private researchers.** Professional researchers can be hired to search for you.

30. **The Internet on the computer.** (Read Chapter 11, "Computers," for more information.)

31. **LDS Church Family History Library** in Salt Lake City, Utah. Family history centers are located around the world in LDS chapels. (See Chapter 6, "Books of Remembrance and Genealogical Records," for more information.)

Look for anything else that shows family names, dates, places, events, and relationships. Most important, follow the Spirit. I have heard of many cases in which the Spirit has directed attention to one slight clue or thought. Many times one document can lead to another. Pray and follow the inspiration you will receive. The Lord wants us to do our family histories and keep records. He will help and guide us.

A Note on Determining Accuracy

There are many items that can be confused in family history information. For help in becoming aware of potential problem areas, please read the section on "problems to be aware of" in Chapter 6, "Books of Remembrance and Genealogical Records."

BOOKS OF REMEMBRANCE AND GENEALOGICAL RECORDS

"Those of you who have worked at your genealogies, who realize the importance of the work and have felt the excitement that comes from tying families together and learning of your noble heritage, need to share that excitement with others."

EZRA TAFT BENSON

A Book of Remembrance should contain all your vital statistical and genealogical information. This is where you can go to find important dates and events gathered in one spot. The information falls into two categories: fixed and current. "Fixed information" concerns the past—genealogy, histories, photos, and documents of your ancestors. "Current information," which deals with your living family, requires frequent updating. I am still adding birth certificates, documents, and family histories to my Book of Remembrance.

What Should I Include?

My list of what to include in a Book of Remembrance may be different from yours—that's okay. My definition is not law; it's simply based on what seems to make sense to me. Here is where I put my four-generation pedigree charts, family group sheets, and any other genealogical records—photos, certificates, stories, histories—concerning ancestors in the past four generations in my own line and that of my husband. The prophets have asked that we be accountable for at least four generations, so I feel this is a good stopping point. If you have the room to add more generations, do! For me, any genealogical information past my four generations simply goes into a genealogy book.

This is also where I put my family's birth, blessing, baptism, confirmation, and priesthood ordination certificates. I keep the originals of our patriarchal blessings here. (For everyday use I have a photocopy that I can underline and mark on.) I have included a photocopy of our wedding certificate (the original hangs framed on the wall) and my husband's priesthood lineage and mission papers. Because of the importance of the documents in this book, I keep it in a fireproof box. If you don't have access to one, you may want to keep your valuable original documents in a safe place and put photocopies in your Book of Remembrance. Whatever the case, this should be the place where you keep any important certificates and documents. If you don't have a "spiritual experience" category section in your personal history, you may wish to add your spiritual experiences here. This is the book in which I keep my chronological history of my life and a written copy of my testimony of the gospel.

Once a year, around April general conference time, my extended family holds a "Family Conference on Records." Each individual family brings copies of updated family group sheets for everyone, showing changes in birth, endowment, marriage, or death information. This is also a good time to get people to reminisce and write about events to add to family members' histories. Somehow, if you have a set date for these things, they will get done.

To recap, then, here is a list of things you may wish to include in your Book of Remembrance:

>Genealogical charts and records
>Family histories
>Personal histories
>Old photos of ancestors

Birth certificates
Blessing certificates
Baptism and confirmation certificates
Patriarchal blessings
Priesthood ordination certificates
Mission calls, releases, and certificates
Immigration papers
Citizenship papers
Adoption papers
Wedding announcements
Marriage certificates
Military records
Obituaries
Death certificates
Photos or rubbings of gravestones
Wills
Any letters or transactions that are important to posterity
Current family photos (remember, this is not a scrapbook, but some photos are important—for example, I like to include one photo of the blessing, baptism, or wedding day with the certificate)

Along with these documents and certificates, it would be nice to write some feelings. For example, instead of just having your baptism certificate there alone, think how meaningful it would be to have a paragraph or two telling how you felt at your baptism. Include a little summary about your wedding day with your marriage certificate. These feelings add personality and warmth to the documents.

Many people complain that they don't have copies of old photos of their ancestors. It seems as though there is always someone in the family who has access to photographs but won't give them up. If there is a negative available, that is your best source of a copy. However, don't worry if there isn't. It is very easy now to get quality photocopies made from original photographs. The black-and-white copies that I have seen look almost as good as the originals. A good copy store can also photocopy onto acid-free paper and enlarge a small photo or crop to make an individual photo out of a group shot. Color copies look almost as good as originals and can be made very easily as well.

Another wonderful way to make copies of documents and photos is to use a computer scanner. This will be discussed in more detail in Chapter 11, "Computers."

Putting It Together

In the past, the most common genealogy pages were 8½ by 14 inches. The standard sheets now are 8½ by 11 inches, a size that better accommodates the computers so widely used in genealogy today. This size is also nice because it allows you to use a standard three-ring binder as your Book of Remembrance. As was discussed in Chapter 2, use good quality, acid-free paper. Acid-free sheet protectors of polyethylene or polypropelene should also be used. Make sure that adhesives are archival quality as well. For an original certificate, it is best not to use any adhesives at all—simply slide it into a sheet protector with a card-stock paper behind it for support. If you need to attach it, use acid-free mounting corners.

The nice thing about a Book of Remembrance is that once it is assembled, it usually doesn't take much time to keep it current.

Compiling Genealogical Information

Members of The Church of Jesus Christ of Latter-day Saints feel a special urgency to find their ancestors in order to ensure that their temple work is done for them. But I feel it is also important to trace our ancestors just to find out who we are. If any of your ancestors had lived in a different city, or married someone different, you wouldn't be you! Who are these people who have made you what you are genetically today? Tracing traits that you have inherited can be exciting.

Genealogy is like a never-ending jigsaw puzzle. Unless you have traced all your genealogical lines back to Adam, there will always be work you can do. And the more you work on it, the more thrilling it becomes. Here is a step-by-step outline of how to obtain genealogical information:

1. Begin by filling out a pedigree chart and family group sheets. A pedigree chart records information on the people in four generations: you, your parents, grandparents, and great-grandparents. A family group sheet records information about one set of parents and the children in their family. Sources of information should also be recorded here. Fill out a family group sheet for each married couple on your pedigree chart.

2. Start with yourself and work backwards. An important rule in genealogy is to go from the known to the unknown. Let what you know lead you to what you don't know. For example, facts about your parents' lives will give you clues to your grandparents' lives. This way you can dig deeper and deeper into the past. Decide what you want to learn, following one line or area at a time. Identify everything you can about your family. Recall information by yourself, and then go to other living relatives to see what they know. Record dates and places as accurately as you can. Any unverified information should be traced to a credible source. Conflicting information should be noted and traced.

3. Chapter 5 of this book, "Family Histories," lists several sources for obtaining genealogical information under the subhead "Writing Histories for Others." These sources can be beneficial in filling in the gaps in your information. Another genealogical source is the Internet, discussed in Chapter 11, "Computers." The LDS Church has some excellent booklets that take you step by step through finding ancestors. Contact the family history leaders in your local LDS ward or stake for help.

The Family History Library

If you have chosen the Family History Library in Salt Lake City, Utah, as a source, you can work with a collection of easy-to-use computer files and programs called FamilySearch®. The Family History Library has the world's largest collection of genealogical information. Additionally, family history centers are located in LDS chapels around the world; here you can request and look up a lot of information from the Family History Library. These are good places to start.

The FamilySearch® system currently has six main files:

1. Ancestral File™
2. International Genealogical Index™
3. Family History Library Catalog™
4. Social Security Death Index
5. Military Death Index
6. Temple Ready™ Index

1. The Ancestral File™ is one of the first sources you will want to check for information. This is a collection of pedigree and family group records that people throughout the world have submitted to the Family History Department of the LDS Church. It contains names along with dates and places of birth, marriage, and death.

You can submit your own family records to this file, as well as make corrections to any errors you find. This file also contains the names and addresses of those who contributed to the file so that you can contact them for further research if you wish. Remember that this file is not original information. It is a collection of records submitted by others. For this reason, there can be errors. Make sure you double-check your sources.

You can make printed copies of these records or copy them to diskette for use on a personal computer.

2. The International Genealogical Index™, often referred to as the IGI, contains millions of names of deceased persons from around the world. It does not have any records of living people. The IGI is a list of birth, christening, and marriage dates. It does not join family groups or pedigrees. It also contains dates of ordinances performed in LDS temples.

Many names in the IGI come from vital records from the early 1500s to 1885. Other names are submitted by members of the LDS Church.

3. The Family History Library has thousands of histories, which are a rich source of genealogical information, photos,

biographical sketches, and stories. The Family History Library Catalog™ describes those histories, plus census and birth records, church registers (which include information on christenings, baptisms, confirmations, marriages, and burials), immigration records, military records, books, microfilms, and microfiche that are located in the Family History Library. Virtually everything that is in the library is cataloged here. The records described in the catalog come from all over the world.

A search of the Family History Library Catalog™ will show all the family histories that include references to other families' surnames. For example, if I were to search for my surname, the catalog could tell me all the books and publications that have reference to my name.

The Family History Library Catalog™ does not contain the actual documents, but rather descriptions of them, such as the author, title, format, notes, contents, and publication information. A call number is used for each record in the Family History Library. This number tells you where to locate the record in the library; you must search through the books and films described in the catalog yourself. You also use this call number when you order copies through a family history center.

4. The Social Security Death Index has a list of 39.5 million deceased people who had social security numbers and whose deaths were reported to the Social Security Administration. It does not contain records of deaths of people who never received Social Security payments, or people whose deaths were not reported to the Social Security Administration. It does not contain records of living persons.

This record can help to identify birth and death dates, but not places. It does, however, identify the place where death benefits were sent, which could help you locate other living relatives. It will also identify the last place of residence where a person's Social Security checks were sent, which may help you locate a death certificate or an obituary. The state where the ancestor was issued a Social Security number can be identified, as well as the number itself. This may help you get more information directly from the Social Security Administration.

The index, which is updated yearly, mainly covers deaths after 1962. Some records, however, are as early as 1937. You do not need your ancestor's Social Security number to use this index. The index will not give information about the deceased's spouse, parents, children, or other information in the Social Security file.

5. The Military Index is helpful if you have relatives who died (or were declared dead) while serving in the military in Korea or Vietnam from 1950 to 1975. This record does not contain any information on individuals who died in any other war or military conflict. (See appendix for other military sources.)

The Military Index can find a birthdate but not a birthplace. A death date is listed along with the country where the individual died. The person's home residence at the time of enlistment, race, rank, service number, and branch of service are listed. For soldiers in Vietnam, the date their tour of duty started, religious affiliation, and marital status will also be listed. Information concerning the person's spouse, parents, or children will not be listed.

6. For members of The Church of Jesus Christ of Latter-day Saints, the Temple Ready™ computer program helps prepare ancestors' names to be submitted for vicarious temple ordinances. Arrange to meet with a ward family history consultant, who will provide you with any help you need in preparing your diskette to take to the temple.

The Family History Library also has records dealing with geographical, historical, or cultural information. They include local histories, gazetteers, modern and old maps, postal guides, language dictionaries, "how-to" books, and guidebooks. By searching these records you may learn more about the area where your ancestors lived.

Problems to Be Aware Of

Determining accurate dates. Dates are one of the most common things to be confused in genealogical records. There are several reasons for this. One major reason, I think, is that an inaccurate date is hard to notice right away. For example, the spelling checker on my computer will recognize a misspelled word, but it doesn't know if a date is wrong or right. My eye, too, can easily pick up a misspelled word, but a date with an incorrect number looks fine.

In the book *Do People Grow on Family Trees?* Ira Wolfman explains that his grandfather's tombstone says that he was born on November 16, 1879. His death certificate says he was born on November 25, 1882, and his citizenship papers say the date was November 25, 1881. Which one is correct? Well, when you think about it, the only place that his grandfather personally wrote the date was on the citizenship papers. Obviously, he didn't fill out his own death certificate or carve his own tombstone. (Tombstone dates are especially problematic, as they are difficult to correct once carved wrong, so they should always be verified.) Who knows what mistakes a grieving person will make at such a time? In this case, the logical assumption is that the correct date would be the one that the grandfather wrote.

The proper way to write dates for genealogical research is day-month-year. Written this way, 8 June 1918 looks like 08/06/18. However, it seems as though the majority of Americans write month-day-year. This same date would then be 06/08/18. If you didn't know the writer's style, you might assume that June 8 was August 6. If you can, I think it is much less confusing to use the abbreviation for the month, such as 30 Mar 1913.

Some people have made themselves younger than they really were. Immigrant ship tickets were cheaper for younger children. Sometimes parents would "subtract" as much as two years off a child's age to get a cheaper ticket. Other people didn't like being forty, so they said that they were thirty-eight at the immigration station. Still others made themselves older so that they could travel by themselves: a fifteen-year-old boy might pose as an eighteen-year-old.

Some people really didn't know when they were born. Many

American states didn't keep birth records until after 1900. In some countries dates were often incomplete or nonexistent.

Accuracy with names. Many immigrants changed or shortened their names after arriving in the United States. *Mastromarino* might have been shortened to *Marino,* for instance. Some were even assigned new names because the immigration officers felt there were too many people with the same surname. Often these names have no connection at all to the family's original surname—one family I know of had the name *Elquist* changed to *Anderson.* Names were changed in military groups for the same reasons. If you are having difficulty or have come to a dead end, check for this possibility.

Always look for the many ways a name could have been spelled. Many recorders spelled names according to sound. Don't eliminate possibilities because of a minor change in spelling: *Anne* could be *Ann; Johanson* could be *Johnson.* Be sure to check for nicknames and abbreviations, such as *Ben* for *Benjamin, Nick* for *Nicolas.* Through the years some surnames have been known to have twenty-five different variations in spelling. And remember that a woman may be listed under her maiden name. When filling out a pedigree chart, write the surname in all capital letters. This makes scanning for names easier.

Most original documents are handwritten. If you cannot read a letter, you will need to search the records very carefully to see how the writer made certain letters. Some words will be obvious; use those to study the writer's style. Libraries may have a handwriting style card for the period you are studying.

Accuracy of place names. In order to avoid confusion with names of places, always write them in this order: City/township, County, State, Country. (For example, Salt Lake City, Salt Lake County, Utah, United States of America.)

Multiple submissions. More than one person may have contributed information to some sources you are checking, which may result in discrepancies and duplication. Go to original sources where possible.

Dead ends. Don't be discouraged when you come to a dead

end. Start on another line. Be patient; often a clue comes from an unexpected source.

More Than a Pedigree Chart

Once you've found your ancestors, it's fun to do more with the names than just have them on paper. Family trees can be displayed in many creative ways. I've seen beautiful family trees done using photos on a picture of a tree. Others have been done using embroidery, paint, or appliqué. I've also seen family trees on quilts and tablecloths. My brother made a beautiful calligraphy tree for my family. The fact that it was done with his own hand makes it even more special to me.

In a booklet called "The Living Family Tree," Marie Schreiner gives suggestions for unusual family trees. Some of them are:

1. An artifact tree. Make a tree using items that relate to each person: a lock of hair, a fingerprint, a baby tooth, and so on.

2. Meaningful shape tree. The Schreiners, whose father was a Tabernacle organist, have a "tree" that lists family names on organ pipes. A family who likes to read could use books on a shelf. An airplane outline could be used for the family of a pilot.

3. Handprint tree. One woman created a tree out of eighty-one handprints. Relatives sent tracings of their hands and she cut the shapes using different shades of fabric for each generation. Embroidered on each handprint was the person's name and a number indicating the order of birth. The handprints were then attached to a quilt.

Family Games

What better way could there be to get to know your ancestors than by playing a game? Doing this at an extended family get-together is not only informative, but can be a bonding time as well.

Bingo. Photocopied faces of ancestors can be made into Bingo cards. Instead of calling out numbers, as in regular Bingo, the one in charge asks questions—for example, "Who received a

Ph.D. from Columbia University in New York?" A marker would then be placed on the face of the relative who did.

Trivia. Here a list of questions is prepared like that suggested for the Bingo game. People are divided into teams and asked the questions one by one. The team who answers the most questions wins. (All kinds of variations can be used; you may wish to move markers around a board, or have members from each team compete head-to-head with each other.)

Crossword puzzles. Family names can be hidden in a crossword puzzle or word search. The clues to the names are facts about the ancestors.

Concentration. Have a photo of an ancestor on one card and an interesting fact about him or her on the matching card. Lay the cards out, face down, in a grid pattern and take turns flipping over two cards to find a match. You could also play by matching husbands and wives.

"This is your life." At a family home evening, a family member who has been assigned an ancestor gives a "This is your life" presentation about him or her. You could even dress up as the person and tell about "yourself."

Kissin' Cousins

Have you ever wondered what a second or third cousin was? Or what about a first cousin once removed? (How do you get a cousin removed, anyway?) When my nephew and his wife had a baby, I wondered what that made me, a great-aunt? (I've always been a wonderful and great aunt!)

The definition of *cousin* is any relative who is descended from a common ancestor with you, but is not your brother or sister. Adding a "second," "first," or "once removed" makes the term more specific or formal.

A first cousin has two of the same grandparents as you. These are the sons and daughters of your aunts and uncles. Other terms for a first cousin are *own, full,* and *cousin-german.*

Second cousins are the children of first cousins. They have the same two great-grandparents.

A third cousin has the same great-great-grandparents as you do. This goes on and on. We have eighth and ninth cousins and more somewhere out there.

Adding a "removed" to the term means that you come from different generations. For example, the child of your first cousin is your first cousin once removed. So, my nephews and nieces are my children's first cousins. The children of my nephews and nieces are my children's first cousins once removed.

If this is confusing to you, take a look at the chart on the following page. Follow the accompanying instructions, and soon you'll be an expert at the "who's who in our family" game!

How to Use the Relationship Chart

1. Figure out what ancestor you have in common with another relative (top left corner of the chart).

2. On the top row of the chart, find your relationship with the common ancestor.

3. On the first vertical column of the chart, find your relative's relationship with the common ancestor.

4. Trace down and across the grid to find where you meet. That is the formal term for your relationship. That person is your _____. (Fill in the blank with the words from that square on the chart.)

Example: Ceciley and Tessa have a common ancestor in Grandma June Young. Ceciley follows across the top to the square labeled *grandchild*. Tessa reads down the left-hand side to *great-grandchild*. As we pull them together, we see that formally the two cousins are first cousins once removed.

RELATIONSHIP CHART

YOUR RELATIONSHIP TO COMMON ANCESTOR

COMMON ANCESTOR	CHILD	GRANDCHILD	GREAT GRANDCHILD	GREAT GREAT GRANDCHILD	THIRD GREAT GRANDCHILD
CHILD	BROTHER/SISTER	UNCLE/AUNT	GREAT UNCLE/AUNT	GREAT GREAT UNCLE/AUNT	THIRD GREAT UNCLE/AUNT
GRANDCHILD	NEPHEW/NIECE	FIRST COUSIN	FIRST COUSIN ONCE REMOVED	FIRST COUSIN TWICE REMOVED	FIRST COUSIN THREE TIMES REMOVED
GREAT GRANDCHILD	GRAND NEPHEW/NIECE	FIRST COUSIN ONCE REMOVED	SECOND COUSIN	SECOND COUSIN ONCE REMOVED	SECOND COUSIN TWICE REMOVED
GREAT GREAT GRANDCHILD	GREAT GRAND NEPHEW/NIECE	FIRST COUSIN TWICE REMOVED	SECOND COUSIN ONCE REMOVED	THIRD COUSIN	THIRD COUSIN ONCE REMOVED
THIRD GREAT GRANDCHILD	GREAT GREAT GRAND NEPHEW/NIECE	FIRST COUSIN THREE TIMES REMOVED	SECOND COUSIN TWICE REMOVED	THIRD COUSIN ONCE REMOVED	FOURTH COUSIN

YOUR RELATIVE'S RELATIONSHIP TO ANCESTOR

PHOTOGRAPHS, SLIDES, AND NEGATIVES

"A good snapshot stops a moment from running away."

E U D O R A   W E L T Y

Say "cheese"! I think almost everyone owns at least *some* photographs—I even met a homeless man who had a sentimental photo tucked carefully away in his pocket. Photos come in all styles and formats—everything from the four-for-a-dollar, photobooth specials to professional portraits—and they vary in sentimental and monetary value. Some photos are meant to last a day, while others are wanted for a lifetime and beyond. For example, I have very few photos of my grandparents, so those I do have are priceless to me. And I also have a lot of photos of silly things that don't mean much to me at all. In any case, I'd have to say that my photo collection is one of my most priceless possessions. I think most people feel the same way: When asked what they would grab in an emergency evacuation, many people mention their photographs.

I love to take photographs. I love to look at them, and I love to share them with others. I have never regretted having a photo of an event or been frustrated that I had too many photos of my children! On the contrary—it seems as though every time I take a photo of an occasion, there is always someone asking, "Can I have a copy?" Photos make the past real in a way that nothing else can. I have heard that children will remember an event from even a very young age if they have a photo to remind them of it.

I believe this is true, because I have recollections from every childhood event for which I have a photo. Photos are fairly inexpensive and easily available; we should never hesitate to take a photograph.

The study of photography is a very large subject, one upon which volumes have been written. Many college and community education courses are offered in this area as well. This chapter will barely make a dent in the subject of photographic techniques, ideas, and equipment, but I do hope to cover the basics and answer questions for the average reader. If you want to know more, the bibliography in the back of the book has some great books for you to study.

What Should I Photograph?

Cameras are commonly found at weddings, birthday celebrations, vacations, and graduations. But what about the common, everyday activities of families working, laughing, and crying together? Candid shots of these day-to-day experiences are usually my favorite photos.

Following is a list of categories of different photos to take. Of course, this list is not all-encompassing, but perhaps it will help you think of ideas appropriate to your own situation. More important, it can remind you to have your camera ready and with you at these times. (And, of course, always have film on hand.)

Candid shots. I love professional portraits and have them taken every year, but candid snapshots often depict the personality of the subject better. I remember going to a professional studio for portraits when I was a teenager. The photographer kept tilting my chin at an awkward angle; then he told me to freeze. The next thing out of his mouth was, "Now just act natural." The portraits are nice, but they don't show my typical self.

Take candid shots of people doing the common things they do. For example, my husband is not much of a night person and is always falling asleep on the floor. I have lots of silly photos of him asleep—an accurate, typical portrayal that a professional portrait could never depict.

My kids love to make huts out of blankets and chairs in the living room. Someday when the kids are gone and my living room is spotless, I know I'll cherish the photos of those huts and the memories they bring to mind.

Candid shots of everyday life will be enjoyable to future generations. Changing a tire, cooking, eating, playing games, doing laundry, and washing dishes are not glamorous activities, but there is value in showing life as it is. I'd love a photo of my grandmother washing clothes with a washboard—someday our activities will be just as interesting to someone else.

Have your camera always loaded with film and in a place where you can easily grab it when those candid, spur-of-the-moment, unexpected times come. A couple of summers ago, when we were sitting outside our cabin, a brown bear came strolling by about twenty feet from us! I'm so glad that my camera was there and ready to go.

Some people complain that whenever they pull out the camera, the kids start acting silly. My children are so used to me taking snapshots of them that they hardly blink; it's no big deal to them. If you take photos often, your family will relax and begin to just ignore it.

Family. This suggestion may seem obvious, but I offer it anyway: Make sure you have good, current photos of your family members. When my friend's dad died, they had to use a photo that was twenty years old for the obituary. There were no useable photos of him that were any more recent.

Pets. To many people, their pets are part of the family. Even if you don't feel that way, it's still nice to have photos of the pets you have owned and loved.

First-time events. We all have firsts, and it's nice to have photos to help us remember them. Some first moments are: first steps, the first day of school, first date, first day driving, first time skiing, and so on.

Lasts. Just as we have firsts, we have lasts. Children have the last day with a bottle or diaper. We may have the last dinner before going away to college or on a mission, the last day before moving or getting married, the last day at a school or in a job.

Before and after. I love these! Haircuts make good before-and-after photos, as do children's teeth coming out and growing in. Landscaping jobs and home remodeling are interesting too.

Disasters. Although at the time you may just want to forget the flood, fire, or mudslide, down the road you will most likely want to remember it, especially to show its effects to others.

Teachers, leaders, and coaches. One of my favorite photos is of my daughter and "her bishop." School, music, church, and dance teachers can be forgotten without a photo. Usually sports teams take team photos, but if they don't, you should! What about the school bus driver, your home and visiting teachers, and your neighbors?

Talents and hobbies. Have a photo taken when you're doing what you like to do: making pottery, gardening, playing the guitar, working on a car, sewing, playing basketball. Have someone photograph you standing with your prized possessions or collectibles.

Programs and events. I remember that I was the announcer at my first-grade school program. Oh, how I wish I had a photo of that event! Dance and music recitals, plays, parades, school and church programs are special times to be remembered with a photo.

Schoolwork. Often children bring home big art projects or science experiments from school. After a while there is no space to keep the salt-dough volcano or the Styrofoam model of the solar system. Take photos of the children holding their works; then it is easier to throw them away. Big pieces of artwork can also be taken to the photocopier and "shrunk" to fit a scrapbook.

Homes. A great history can be told by taking photos of not only the outsides of the homes you live in but the insides as well. For some reason, someone took a photo of my bedroom when I was in college. It was a disastrous mess! At the time it was embarrassing to see, but now it's really fun. I can see all the things that I was doing and what I was working on then. If the room had been clean, I wouldn't know about the textbooks I was studying from, the clothes I wore back then, or other interesting things about my life at that time. (Clean rooms are nice too, though.)

I'm grateful for the one photo we have of the house in which my mother was born. That house has since been torn down. My dad's childhood home is still standing, and I have recently taken a photo of it, but it would be nice to have one from when he lived there. I'm sure it has changed.

Special and frequented places. Take photos of church buildings, places of employment, schools, the hospital you were born in, or just places where you "hang out." I have a great photo of the bench where my husband and I met.

Cars. I wish so much that I had photos of my family's old cars. My dad's 1947 and 1954 Pontiacs, his 1952 Chevrolet, and the 1956 Imperial were such classics, and the only memory I have of them is in my head. We don't stop to consider that the cars we drive today will be collectors' items someday. Take their picture!

Progression. These types of photos show growth and progress. My daughter loves to see the progressive pregnant shots of me carrying her. I wore the same dress once a month for a growth photo. (Wearing the same dress will result in more accurate pictures than if you change clothes, because each different outfit affects how large you look.) I held a paper with the date in my hand to show how many weeks or months along I was in the pregnancy.

Progressive shots of us building our cabin have been enjoyable as well. We have taken photos from ground-level dirt to foundation, framing, and finishing. In big projects, photos can help you look back and see how far you really have come. They offer encouragement when you know there is still a lot of work ahead.

Friends. My friends are dear to me and I love having photos of them. I'm sad to say that I have had friends move away without my ever having taken photos of them. Make sure you get group photos of friends as well. If you are in a presidency or a committee, get a group shot. You'll be so glad you did.

"A Day in the Life of . . ." One woman told me that each year on her children's birthdays she takes lots and lots of photos throughout the day: first thing in the morning, during breakfast, at school, after school at work, doing chores, playing, and so on. She then puts them together in a book called "A Day in the Life of (child's name)." The children can look back to the books from past years and see the changes in their lives.

"A day in the life" could be good for any age or occasion. What a great idea for a missionary or student away at college!

Holidays and special occasions. Birthdays and Christmas are the two most popular photo-taking days. Don't forget to photograph the Halloween costumes, Thanksgiving dinner, the Valentine presents, Easter baskets and bonnets, the New Year's Eve party, or the Fourth of July barbecue. Baby blessings, baptisms, and priesthood ordinations are special occasions to be remembered. And I have never met a bride yet who thought she had too many photos of her wedding day.

Some think that cameras are taboo at funerals, but I am grateful for all the photos taken at my father's funeral. I spent most of the day in numbness, and the photos remind me of who was there. It was also one of those rare times when the whole family was together.

Gifts. Arranging your birthday, Christmas, or wedding presents together and then taking a photo is a great memory reminder. It's fun to see what you got for Christmas ten years ago!

Some Hints

1. Make sure you get into some photos yourself! It seems as though there tends to be one member of the family who usually takes the photos. Make sure that person gets in a photo now and then too. My friend's mother was always the one with the camera. They didn't realize this was true until she died and they

couldn't find any photos of her. Using a tripod with a camera that has a timer is a good way to get everyone in a photo.

2. Some cameras put the date automatically on the photo so you will know when it was taken. If you don't have this feature, keep a log of the dates when you take photos. A typical entry might read: "Ceciley and Joseph sitting on the porch swing, June 19, 1996." Another idea is to write the date on a card or paper and have someone in the photo hold it.

3. At special events, have as many people taking photos as possible. A man told me of his wedding-day catastrophe: The photographer lost all the rolls of film from that day in a fire! Having several photographers (some amateur) not only insures you against a disaster, but gives different perspectives. Some of my favorite photos from my wedding were not the posed shots taken by the professional photographer, but candid ones that my brother took. Several people took photos that day and each captured the event differently.

4. If you find yourself out of town without your camera, buy a disposable one. These cameras won't give you quite the quality of photo you might be used to, but they aren't bad—surely better than nothing. And the price isn't too much more than you'd pay for a roll of film. It's also fun to get disposables now and then for the children to use. I'm amazed at some of the shots my six-year-old has taken!

5. Respect others when taking photos. There are some people who *really* do not like to have their picture taken. As wonderful as photos are, never force anyone to participate who doesn't want to.

6. When taking landscape photos, it is always more interesting to have a person in them. This can also help date the photo and give perspective.

7. Sometimes I love to capture a lot of what is going on in the background of my photos. At other times I like a very simple background. As far as background is concerned, the most important thing is to pay attention to objects that might look silly, such as plants that seem to be growing out of the top of people's heads.

8. Don't forget that it's all right to rotate the camera. Often a vertical orientation fits the subject better than a horizontal one.

Photographic Papers

There are two kinds of paper used in photographic processing that are important to know about at this point: fiber-based paper and resin-coated or RC paper. It is easy to tell the difference simply by examining the back of the photo. The back of a fiber-based photo feels like paper; the back of a resin-coated photo is slick and shiny. Color photos, generally speaking, are developed on RC paper—exceptions to this are extremely rare.

Early in photographic history, developers understood the importance of using a good quality rag paper for photo processing. Through the years this paper was improved, and it was generally felt that if properly developed and cared for, these photos would be very stable and permanent. There are some concerns, however, with fiber-based prints. Differences in moisture absorption between the paper base and the emulsion layer cause curling. The paper absorbs moisture so well that it becomes limp and weak. Washing and drying times in the processing cycle are long.

Efforts were made in the late 1960s to make a paper with less absorption capacity and a greater resistance to tearing and curling. The water-resistant, resin-coated paper was the result. This paper is composed of a basic photographic paper coated on the top and bottom with a plastic layer of polyethylene. The photographic emulsion is then applied over the polyethylene. It is far easier to process and wash a resin-coated paper than a fiber-based one. The problems of curling and tearing are also minimized with the resin-coated paper.

Although an improvement in some areas, the early resin-coated prints had problems in others. A pigment added to the polyethylene absorbed light and promoted cracking of the resin layer. By the late 1970s, "stabilized" RC papers were being used; they contained an antioxidant that eliminated the cracking but tended to cause a yellowish stain. This too was eventually corrected.

Even with the advances and the advantages of resin-coated paper, many photographers still feel it is an inferior paper. However, Jim Reilly, the director of the Image Permanence Institute at the Rochester Institute of Technology, says that technology has removed any concerns about RC paper. At this time there is no longer any technical basis for believing that all RC prints are greatly inferior to fiber-based prints.

Black-and-White versus Color Photographs

Many people have asked me why their grandparents' hundred-year-old photos look better than their own fifty-year-old collections. Much of this has to do with the difference between black-and-white and color photos, especially if those color shots were taken in the fifties and sixties. In a black-and-white photo, silver is used to create the image. Metals such as silver are stronger against outside influences than the organic dyes used in color images. And, again, old black-and-whites were developed on fiber-based paper that was more stable than the early resin-coated paper. Properly developed and cared for, an old black-and-white photograph can last for a hundred years without any deteriorative changes.

Although a black-and-white image is more permanent than a color one, color photography is still wonderful. Approximately 90 percent of the 14 billion snapshots taken every year in the United States are in color. Unfortunately, color film is generally not as stable as black-and-white film. The chemicals used in color film processing alter the color dyes over time. Environmental factors also accelerate this deteriorative process. There is really no way to restore the altered dye image once it has deteriorated. Sad but true, most color photographs are not permanent and will fade even in dark storage. The day they are developed they start deteriorating. How much or how quickly they will fade depends on a number of factors, including (1) the type of film used, (2) how the photograph was processed or developed, (3) environmental and storage conditions, and (4) handling, care, and treatment procedures. Even though color photographs inherently fade, there are some things we can do to slow the process. Black-and-white film that is developed on a resin-coated polyester base (as most color photos are) will deteriorate over time as well. The suggestions in the remainder of this chapter would be applicable for black-and-white film too.

Types of Film

Image permanence has been receiving a lot of attention in the past decade. Competition among film manufacturers has greatly intensified, and the consumer is the beneficiary. Everyone is making great strides in the improvement of color stability and image permanence. Three dyes are used in the developing process: cyan, magenta, and yellow. Different films carry different dye stability levels. Under certain circumstances, yellow may fade faster than cyan, for example. The opposite may be true of a different film. Kodak has traditionally been the leading company in the quality of film. Recently, however, Fujicolor papers have shown a better dye stability and much lower rates of yellowish stain than Kodak papers. Of course, this could all be different by the time this book goes to press!

Most manufacturers include a fading warranty on their color film packages. One reads, "Since color dyes may change over time, this product will not be replaced for, or otherwise warranted against, any change in color."

Seven leading manufacturers of photographic materials are Kodak, Fuji, Agfa, Konica, 3M, Ilford, and Polaroid. Check with a professional in your area to find the best film for your camera and needs. Remember to be a wise consumer. Products change, and the one that is the best today may not be tomorrow. For more information, read Henry Wilhelm's book, *The Permanence and Care of Color Photographs: Traditional and Digital Color Prints, Color Negatives, Slides, and Motion Pictures.* This has a myriad of charts and graphs to identify color stability of different types of films.

Processing and Developing

To understand the developing process, you need to know what a photograph consists of. A photograph is made up of two parts. The *support* or *base* is any material that supports the emulsion. It can be glass, plastic film, paper, or resin-coated paper. This is the nonimage side of a photographic print or negative. The *image-building emulsion material* may be made of silver, color dyes, and/or pigment particles. It is usually suspended in a gelatin layer. When the silver salts are exposed to light, they turn into minute grains of black and metallic silver that form an image. In a color photo, after the silver grains are developed to a black-and-white image, the developer color couplers are introduced, forming a color dye image on the film. The silver is then bleached and washed away. Dyes left on the film are very volatile and sensitive to fading. In a black-and-white photo, the silver stays on the image; this makes a black-and-white photo more stable than one with color dyes.

Chemicals are used to develop the silver image and/or couple with color dyes. The developed image is then made light-fast, or stabilized, by immersing it in "fixers." Hopefully, the photograph is then thoroughly washed to remove any chemical residue. If there is insufficient washing, unexposed silver salts and residual chemicals are left on the photo and can have a deteriorative effect on the emulsion layer. Leftover silver salts absorb light, causing images to darken. Other chemical residues cause discoloration.

Unfortunately, a majority of photo labs (especially one-hour labs) wash photos minimally or not at all. Some photos are even rinsed in old, exhausted, contaminated, or nonrecommended chemicals. To preserve your prints from chemical damage, find and use a larger professional lab that will develop to the standards of the American National Standards Institute (ANSI).

Deterioration caused by residual salts and chemicals is prevented if the film is developed archivally. Typical one-hour shops will not develop photos in an archival manner; you will need to check around for a place that will custom-process your photos for you. Archival processing is far more expensive than regular commercial developing. However, from time to time, it is worth having archival prints made, especially of important occasions.

Black-and-white prints may be made to an archival standard if they are processed on 100 percent double-weight, fiber-based paper using only fresh chemicals and a lengthy water wash. In this process, all unused salts and chemicals are completely removed. Additionally, a protective toner is added to shield the silver layer. This will protect the photo from other contaminants and deterioration. Have the print made with a border around the image. This space acts as a buffer.

Another way to create a long-lasting print is to have a Cibachrome (Ilfochrome) color print made. These can only be made from color slides. Two bases are available: A polyester base is more stable than a resin-coated one. Only a custom lab will make this type of print for you, and it is about four times the cost of a regular reprint, but again, worth it from time to time for the more important images.

The bottom line is this: If you have film from a special occasion, never take it to a cheap, fast photo lab such as those typically found in grocery and drug stores. My friend took photos the day her son was blessed and had them developed at a quick, cheap store. The prints came back with a horrible stripe through them. The negatives had the same line, caused by a scratch created at the time of developing. When you take your film to a custom lab, more caution and time is taken with your film, and you can usually count on more washing time and better chemicals. Yes, it will cost more money, too, but it is well worth it.

For best results, it is important to use your film before the "Develop Before" date printed on the package. Take your film to be developed as soon as possible after you finish exposing the roll. Normal deterioration characteristics that occur with age can be slowed down if you do this.

Environment

All photographic material is organic, and so it is affected by its environment. Extremes in temperature, humidity, light, and pollutants accelerate changes in film characteristics and speed deterioration of photos. Unprocessed photographic film is perishable. It's important to keep your unprocessed film in its original package until you are ready to use it. This will help protect it from contaminants. Be aware of the following:

Humidity. All photographic materials are sensitive to high, low, and fluctuating relative humidity. (*Relative humidity* is the measure of how saturated the air is with moisture.) High relative humidity causes the gelatin binder to become soft and sticky, allowing the image to deteriorate. It also speeds up chemical reactions that lead to fading and discoloration. Low relative humidity causes the binder to shrink, crack, and curl. Optimal relative humidity would be about 30 to 40 percent, never higher than 50 percent. Relative humidity is the most critical factor in the deterioration of black-and-white prints and negatives.

Some exterior walls are prone to dampness. Use caution when displaying photographs on these walls, since some of the moisture may migrate to the print. Avoid storing or displaying photos in any damp area such as an unfinished basement or garage.

Temperature. Temperature is the most significant factor affecting the rate of image fading in color prints. The higher the temperature, the faster the deterioration, especially at high humidity levels. In high temperature and humidily, your photos are very susceptible to mold as well. Once active mold infests your photographic materials, it is usually impossible to remove it without damaging the photo (although early stages of mold and fungus can sometimes be brushed off with a soft cotton cloth). Mold tends to develop when the temperature is above 75 or 80 degrees and the humidity greater than 60 percent. Optimal temperature for storing and displaying color photos would be

109

below 68 degrees F. Every 10 degrees F. reduction in temperature will approximately double the life of a color print.

Keep in mind that heat can come from incandescent lights placed too close to a photograph. In an area where photos are kept, use a low-watt bulb (no more than 60 watts). Also, heat from radiators, heat ducts, fireplaces, and even hot cars can damage photos. Photos mounted above a working fireplace look nice, but are being harmed and deteriorated by the heat from the fireplace. Hang only copies there, never originals.

Cycling. Photographs are also damaged by "cycling," fluctuations in temperature and humidity. For example, photos kept in a garage, basement, or attic can undergo temperature swings as radical as 125 degrees F. Cycling allows moisture in and out of the photograph. This promotes chemical deterioration and structural damage. Controlled humidity and temperature will help prevent curled prints, mold, fungus, blotchy stains, and cracked emulsions.

Light. Light is very damaging to photos. I recently took a photo out of a frame that had been sitting on my mother's shelf for years. About half an inch of the photo had been hidden behind the frame all that time and consequently never saw the light. The difference in the brightness and clarity of that half-inch strip was dramatic. The more direct light a photo receives, the faster the image will fade.

Direct sunlight and standard fluorescent light are both strong sources of heat and ultraviolet radiation. Photographs subjected to such light and heat will eventually fade and become structurally weakened. Keep photos at least four feet away from any type of incandescent or fluorescent lights. Never store them in direct sunlight. Some protection can be given by framing the photo behind a filtering acrylic. Filtering sleeves can also be used on florescent tubes to reduce ultraviolet light levels.

I like to make prints of my sentimentally valuable photographs, frame the copies, and store the originals safely away from light and temperature extremes. This way I can enjoy displaying the copies anywhere and not be as concerned about the environment. I have even framed a color photocopy of a print, and it looks great. (See more about framing on pages 173–77.)

Pollutants. All kinds of pollutants can have adverse effects. Fumes from paints and solvents are particularly hard on photographs, even in small quantities. A friend of mine had some photos resting on his dresser in a haphazard way. He moved the dresser out from the wall about three feet to paint the wall. The next day, when the paint was dry, he moved the dresser back against the wall. As the photos shifted, he could see a shadowed line from where they had been lying during the painting. Hydrogen peroxide is generated during the curing of certain paints, and the fumes from the wet paint had faded the photos overnight! Photographs should be removed for at least six weeks from a room that has been painted with an oil-base paint. Water-based latex paints do not release as many oxidants; photographs should be removed from a room being painted with latex paint and left out for twenty-four hours after the painting is finished.

Be cautious of any chemical fumes. Even simple air pollution from car exhausts or the burning of coal and oil can interact with photographic images. Fumes from solvents, cleaners, insecticides, foam-injected insulation, varnishes, shellacs, and even fabric treatments such as permanent press and stain inhibitors all contain formaldehyde or aldehyde derivatives, sulfides, or other agents that can harm unprocessed or processed photographic materials. Certain types of cosmetics such as hair spray can also produce image deterioration.

Soot, ash, dust, and any other particles that may be greasy or abrasive are harmful as well. These often enter our homes through heating and cooling ducts, doors, and windows. Good housekeeping, screens, and filters can help eliminate some of this.

Photocopiers, including laser copiers, produce ozone, which is a bleach. The fumes can accelerate deterioration. It's a good idea never to store photos by these machines, because the light and heat from the copiers are harmful as well.

Insects and rodents. Insects and rodents will eat the gelatin and cellulose in the photographic emulsion. Photos as well as paper are shredded to make nests. Any kind of animal droppings are damaging, causing stains and encouraging fungus growth. Good housekeeping and storing photos in normal living areas will help to eliminate any problems with little critters.

X rays. Unprocessed film is affected by X rays. High doses can fog the film, but several low doses can be damaging as well because the effects of X-ray exposure are cumulative. (Once your photos have been developed, they will not be affected.) High-speed film is especially susceptible to damage from X-ray exposure.

When you travel by airplane, your checked baggage as well as your carry-on bags will be subjected to X-ray examination. A little exposure is expected, but remember that effects are cumulative and excessive amounts can cause an objectionable fog and shadow the images on the film. If your luggage will be X-rayed more than five times, or if you are going to a foreign country where radiation levels for inspection may be higher, there are some things you can do to avoid too much danger.

1. Due to new airport regulations, it is best to not have your camera loaded when flying. When high-level security is in force, opening of cameras at the security gate may be mandatory.

2. Travel with film in a specially made, lead-lined bag. These bags, which look like a polyester lunch sack with a lead liner, will shield your film from any damaging X rays. Be prepared to submit the bag for physical inspection, however, because when it goes through the X-ray machine, nothing will show.

3. Request a visual inspection of your bag instead of X rays. This takes a little longer, so some security personnel may not want to cooperate. Have the camera or film in a bag with not much else to avoid spending too much time.

4. Each time you pack your bag, arrange the contents so that the film is placed in a different position. This will change the direction of X-ray exposure on your film. Placing your bag on the X-ray equipment differently each time will do the same thing.

5. Have the film processed on your trip, before you fly home.

112

6. Carry processing mailers and mail your film home. Mark on the package, "Undeveloped Photographic Film. Please Do Not X-ray." Sometimes, however, mailed packages are X-rayed.

Note: "Walk-through" and handheld electronic devices used to check people through airport security are not X-ray devices and will not affect your film. (This is *exactly the opposite for magnetic tapes,* so if you are transporting those as well, see Chapter 10, "Audio and Video Recordings.")

Storage

The best storage areas for photographic materials are in your normal living areas. Temperature and humidity are easily controlled here and disasters from water damage and "little critters" are minimal in these areas. Basements, attics, and garages are the worst places to store any valuables, especially photographic materials. The environment is not as controlled in these places and they are more susceptible to other outside damages.

Folders, boxes, and protectors. Acids from many standard commercial folders and boxes accelerate the deterioration of photos. Photographs should always be stored in archival folders, envelopes, boxes, or sleeves made of such materials as polyethylene, polypropelene, polyester (Mylar), or Tyvek. Steel filing boxes are fine too. Stay away from any pockets made of polyvinyl chloride (PVC) or acetate. There are many boxes and sheet protectors on the market that claim to be made especially for photos—do not assume they are safe just because they make that claim. Make sure that they are archivally stable and pass the Photographic Activity Test (P.A.T.) of the American National Standards Institute for photographic materials and their storage. The general requirements state that all enclosures should be chemically stable; free of acids, peroxides, and reducible sulfur; with surfaces neither too rough (to scratch) nor too smooth (to cause sticking).

Acid-free paper enclosures are opaque and block incoming light. They are also porous and help prevent the accumulation of moisture. They are a great choice for storage except that it is hard to view the photos while they are in the enclosures, and handling and fingerprints can cause other damage. So I like to use paper enclosures for items that I don't view a lot and that will be stored for a long time.

Use *buffered* paper enclosures for early safety-film negatives and black-and-white negatives and prints. Old, brittle prints on acidic mounts should be stored in buffered enclosures as well. Use *nonbuffered* paper enclosures for color materials, including blueprints (cyanotypes) and albumen prints.

Plastic enclosures allow you to view the image while it is being protected from fingerprints and handling. Unfortunately, under some conditions, plastic enclosures can trap moisture. However, if given proper environmental care, this is rare.

Organization. There is no right or wrong way to organize your photos, negatives, and slides for storage. Whatever works best for you (as long as you use the right materials) is the right way. Some people like to organize their materials chronologically, and others prefer to arrange by subject. The only drawback for subject organization is with negatives. There is often more than one subject on each negative strip. It is not advisable to cut negatives apart, and the strip cannot be stored in two places. (See more about negatives on pages 120–23.)

Choose archival folders, envelopes, sleeves, or boxes (many archival boxes come with dividers for categorizing), label them appropriately, and begin sorting photos either chronologically or by subject. For more ideas, see the section "Getting Organized" in Chapter 8, "Scrapbooks."

Photo albums and scrapbooks are good places in which to store photos once organized. If stored correctly, they can provide a good way to care for photos properly while keeping them accessible to see and enjoy. Many scrapbooks, however, are damaging—especially the so-called "magnetic" ones. The plastic covering is usually made from a nonarchival acetate that gives off gasses that attack the photo image. Also, it completely seals the photo in with the cardboard backing, which is acidic. Read Chapter 8, "Scrapbooks," for more information.

Shelves and cabinets. Do not store photos on shelves or in cabinets that might release harmful vapors or chemicals. Storage cabinets should be made of stainless steel, anodized aluminum, or steel with a powder-coated, baked-on finish. Avoid wooden or ordinary cardboard boxes. Any kind of wood, Masonite, particle board, plywood, or Formica-covered plywood should be avoided, due to the gasses these products emit.

Safety deposit box. Important documents are best stored in a safety deposit box at your bank. These are usually climate controlled and kept dark, which is ideal for your precious photographs.

Avoid direct-image contact. When storing photographs, never allow the image side of a photo to rest against the image side of another photo. The print-to-print contact will allow chemicals to migrate back and forth. This is especially harmful when a poorly processed print is placed next to another photo, or when different types of prints come into contact (for example, a Polaroid instant print next to a Kodacolor print). Direct-image contact can also result in scratching as the prints shift back and forth against each other. And newspaper clippings and other acidic items should never be stored in contact with photos—the migration of chemicals is very harmful.

It's all right for the back of a print to touch the front of another in a stack of photos, but *only* if there is no ink printing on the back. If there is, a small piece of acid-free tissue or paper should be placed between them. This, however, excludes Polaroid photos. They should not be stored touching any other photos. Polaroids are great for quick, easy snapshots, but they should *never* be used for any photo that you want to last. The little pack of chemicals stays with the photo, as do the chemicals on the print that you do not wash off.

Handling and Treatment

Improper handling and treatment of photos is a common problem. The nice thing is that this is one area that we can usually control. If we personally take good care of our photos, using proper techniques and care and some simple common sense, we can increase their life many years.

Touching and handling. Before handling any photo, make sure that your hands are clean. This may seem silly, but fingerprints and smudges are hard to get rid of. Always handle photos by their edges and backs, never touching the emulsion or print side. Old photos should be given support underneath to prevent even slight bending. (Bending can cause the brittle emulsion to crack.) If your photos are valuable or hard to handle by the edges, use clean, lintless cotton gloves. Your hands have a natural oil that transfers easily to photos and can mark and permanently damage them. Sometimes you can't see marks right away, but the oil that is left there attracts other dust and debris that can accelerate deterioration. Think of a crime scene and how fingerprints can be picked up that have been left by the oils in hands. We never notice the prints on our doorknobs and combs, but they're there.

Tape. Never use tape on the image (emulsion) side of a print. The best tapes I know of that are safe to use on the back side of a photo are 3M Scotch no. 415 double-sided tape or single-sided no. 810 Magic Transparent Tape. Ordinary cellophane and masking tapes have rubber-based adhesive that gradually deteriorates, discolors, becomes gooey, and eventually soaks into the photograph. Discoloration can often be noticed in a couple of years. However, the 3M tapes mentioned above are different, being made from a synthetic acrylic polymer adhesive. Aging tests have been conducted to conclude that they will not discolor, stain, or dry out, and the pH is neutral. This tape is really strong and hard to reverse if a lot is used. I stick my photos down with a piece about half an inch long. This way I can get them out easily if needed. There are also transfer tabs of neutral adhesive on the market that are already pre-cut and easy to use.

No matter how good any tape is, *never* use it on the back of a fiber-based print. When you remove the print from the tape, it will tear. Use the tape only on the back of a resin-coated print with a plastic backing.

Corners. Archival corners made from Mylar or paper corners attached with acid-free tape are safe to use. In fact, because tape and glue aren't safe for fiber-based photos, corners are your best alternative for those. Be careful not to purchase photo corners that are vinyl (made with PVC); they are acidic. Corners are easy to use and completely reversible. But for photos that are weak or have fragile, bent, or torn corners, as many old ones do, I do not recommend even archival corners. Too much stress is placed on a small section of the photo, which could cause more tearing or bending. Corners can also be hard on a photo because of the difficulty in putting it back into the corner after it has been taken out. Use caution when doing that! Another alternative is to cut slits in a sheet of acid-free paper and slide the corners of a photo through those.

Protective sheets. Plastic "photo print protector" sheets made from polypropelene or polyethylene can be purchased in common photo sizes. These generally hold six or eight photos per sheet. Old, worn photos can be stored in these sheets to help support the edges. They often have three-ring holes punched in the edges, allowing them to fit nicely inside a scrapbook binder.

Glue. I have seen so many photos ruined from the use of bad glues! Rubber cements are the worst. Their high sulfur content causes chemical stains. A rule of thumb for glue: If it smells, *don't use it!* A water-based glue with a neutral pH is the only safe glue for photos. Never use glue on fiber-based photos. The glue may be okay, but the paper back of the photo is porous and the glue could stain. Also, the photo might tear if you tried to remove it. On a resin-coated photo, a safe glue should be used. The ones that I know are safe are Elmers School Glue and a glue stick made by Avery Dennison. (See more about glue in Chapter 2, "The Right Materials.")

The adhesives on most "magnetic" scrapbook pages are harmful. I am the not-so-proud owner of some photos that have little stripes on them from the glue seeping through to the emulsion layer. Often a strong bond is made and the photos are very difficult to remove without damage. (If this has happened to you, use a hair dryer to help soften the glue before carefully pulling them out.)

Paper clips and rubber bands. Do not use these items with photographs. Paper clips can scratch the surfaces of prints and negatives; they also can leave a permanent bend or crease. Rubber bands contain sulphur, which is harmful to the emulsion layer.

Labeling photos. It is very frustrating to find or inherit photos of people and places you don't recognize. To keep your photos from becoming meaningless, it's important to label and identify them the best you can. Even if you know the subject in the photo, someone else who will see it someday might not.

Writing on the back of photos is the most common way of identifying the dates, people, places, and events pictured. However, care must be taken to not damage the image. Never write on the image side of a photo. For fiber-based prints, a soft No. 2 pencil or carbon pencil may be used to gently write on the back side. Always write near an edge to avoid any problems with the image of the photo. Never push hard enough to leave an impression on the emulsion side. I've seen many photos with indentations on the image from writing on the back. This can be avoided by writing very gently with the photo resting on a hard, smooth surface.

Writing with a pencil on the back of a resin-coated photo is almost impossible, especially with the older photos from about 1968 to 1981. More current photos have backings that accept the pencil better but still not well. You have to press too hard to get an image to appear, and the possibility of making an impression on the other side is very great. Ballpoint pens are unsuitable for the same reason. Recently I have seen a pencil made especially for marking resin-coated photos; I still don't think it works as well as the permanent pens described below, but it is an improvement over a regular No. 2 pencil. Water-based, felt-tip pens are made to write on porous paper surfaces, not photographs. On a fiber-based photo, these inks can bleed through from the back to the emulsion side just like they do on regular paper. On a plastic, nonabsorbent, resin-coated photo, they don't dry fast and will smear and transfer to other photos. Water-based inks also have poor light-fading stability.

A volatile-solvent-based ink may be used on the back of a resin-coated print. These inks are often called "permanent" because they are waterproof and have a better light-fading stability than water-based inks. Henry Wilhem suggests that an India ink such as Koch-I-Nook Rapidomat Ink is the best. However, Pilot Photographic Markers and Sharpie Extra Fine Point Markers are also acceptable. These dry rapidly, are waterproof and permanent, and are more convenient and practical to use than India ink. Remember, although they are safe for a resin-coated print, *never* use these inks on the back of a porous, fiber-based print.

Another way to identify photos is to label them on another piece of paper. Simply write a number on the back of the photo and a corresponding number on an identification list with all the pertinent information about the photo. This way you can give a detailed description of the occasion and even tell a story about it. You could also keep a photocopy of the print with the description to better identify it. This number could also be used to identify and mark the negative.

Sometimes in a large group photo the people are sitting in rows, and it is easy to identify them by row. However, sometimes they are grouped in clusters, making identification more difficult. Here's a way to solve this: Make a photocopy of the photo. Place a thin sheet of tracing paper over the photocopy and trace the outline of each person. Number the people and then make a list by number of who they are.

Make sure when you label a photo that you use both first and last names. If I have a photo on which I have written "Grandpa Young," will the viewer naturally assume that I am talking about *my* grandpa? My dad is a Grandpa Young, and now two of my brothers are Grandpa Youngs. Although it may be obvious to me, in years to come a descendant may not know which Grandpa Young is being shown.

Another example of this is my two sisters-in-law. Both are named Joan Young. One is pronounced "Jo-ann" and the other "Jone," but on paper they are spelled the same. To further complicate things, they both have the middle initial of E. On photos of them, I need to be really specific. Of course, I can tell in a photo who they are, but will descendants be able to?

Another good idea is to label your photos as soon after developing as you can. The longer you wait, the more apt you are to forget dates and events.

Mounting. The mounting of photos is controversial. Some experts feel that vintage prints or photos of value should never be altered. Furthermore, some older photos have stamps of the photographer, past owners, or other important or historical markings on the back side, which will be lost if the photo is mounted. Other experts feel that mounting photos is a good choice since it provides rigidity, prevents wrinkling, and gives some physical protection.

If you choose to mount a photograph, do so archivally. Use acid-free mounting board and choose a dry-mounting technique that is safe. Check with a conservator to ensure that you have the proper materials. The Appendix lists some good suppliers.

Lacquer. Color prints are often lacquered to give a more artistic appearance. Some lacquers can accelerate dye fading, so never lacquer an original or a print you care to have for a long time.

Negatives

I am always surprised when I hear of people who throw their negatives away. Others don't necessarily discard them, but since they don't normally get looked at or displayed, they get lost and forgotten. My negatives are more valuable to me than my prints! They are a wonderful history in and of themselves. Negatives can be printed many times without the colors in the negative fading discernibly. With a negative, I can make copies to enjoy and store a sentimental original safely.

Care should be taken to protect your negatives from dust,

dirt, fingerprints, scratches, and of course the environmental problems that affect photographs. If your negatives have scratches on them, the reprints will have an image of a scratch on them too. Dust is abrasive and can cause scratches, so it is important to guard against it. As mentioned with photos, oils in your hands can cause fingerprints that damage the negative. Always hold them on their edges or wear clean, lintless cotton gloves.

When dealing with negatives, use the same care with regard to humidity, temperature, light, and pollutants as with photos. A relative humidity below 25 percent can lead to brittleness; above 60 percent can stimulate mold. For color negatives, the ideal temperature should really not exceed 50 degrees F. for long-term storage.

The same rules apply to storing negatives as with photos. Keep them in safe archival sleeves, folders, boxes, shelves, and containers. The envelopes they come in after developing are seldom acid-free. There are many types of storage systems made especially for negatives, including envelopes, sleeves, and storage boxes. These are usually provided with spaces to identify or index the negatives. Make sure they are archivally safe. Sleeves should be made of acid-free paper (buffered for black-and-white storage, nonbuffered for color) or plastic such as polyethylene, polypropelene, or Mylar. I like the sleeves that fit in a three-ring binder. As soon as I get a roll of film developed, I carefully slide the negatives into their sleeves and identify the occasions and the dates. I can flip through my binder of negatives and easily find any photo I want to make a reprint of. (This happens all the time. Remember earlier, when I said people are always asking for copies of photos?) I then store this negative binder in a protective fire cabinet.

Never try to conserve space by storing more than one negative in a sleeve or strip. This can cause abrasive scratches. The combined negatives often stick together and damage each other. Negatives and negative strips must be stored individually. Negative strips should also be kept intact, never cut.

Some photo albums have spaces provided next to the print to store the negative. This sounds good in theory: You can easily find the print that corresponds with the negative. This storage method, however, is not such a great idea. I have heard countless disaster stories of photo albums getting ruined. If your negatives are ruined along with the album, then all is lost. But if your negatives are in a different spot, hopefully both album and negatives would not be ruined at the same time, and your photos can be re-created. Very important negatives should be stored in a safety deposit box.

Nitrate film storage. Cellulose-nitrate films were used from the late 1800s to about 1945, when safety film came out. If you have any films or negatives from around that time, they should be looked at very closely. These old films and negatives will have a bluish tint to them and smell like bad honey.

The film industry lost many old movies that were made on this film: The nitrate seeps out and can spontaneously combust. The scary thing is that it doesn't need any kind of match or lighter to catch it on fire—it does it all by itself. These negatives are dangerous to have around your home. They should be stored in buffered paper enclosures and then placed in fireproof cans to be safe. However, because of their makeup, they will disintegrate anyway. It is best to have copy negatives made and to destroy the nitrate films altogether. Put them in your fireplace and watch how fast they catch on fire and disintegrate.

APS storage systems. In the spring of 1996 a new product called Advanced Photo System (APS) was developed to store negatives. This was not designed for archival storage, but rather maximum foolproof loading and convenience. A small print sheet is made to show prints and identify the negatives; then the negatives are stored inside of the film container. I, along with many photographers, have great concern about this type of storage. The emulsion layer is coated with a magnetic surface. Magnetic media are sensitive to change. The negatives have no way to breathe or ventilate. APS should be viewed with skepticism. There is no study as to the longevity of the negative. Until more data is received, use the tried and true methods of negative storage.

Color Slides

Slides, like prints and negatives, are damaged by the environment and poor storage techniques. Use the same guide for pollutants, temperature, and humidity as with photographic prints. Remember, the cooler and drier the better, and keep it consistent.

Light. Obviously, it's impossible to keep slides totally away from direct light—it's the projected light that allows us to show and enjoy them. It's best to avoid projecting a slide for more than 10 seconds at a time to minimize exposure to the intense projector light that causes fading of the dyes. Ektachrome film is less prone to fading under intense projection light, but Ektachrome fades in dark storage faster than Kodachrome slides. Recent studies suggest that Fujichrome is a good compromise.

Storage. As with other photographic materials, stay away from enclosures of vinyl (polyvinyl chloride, PVC), wood cabinets, cardboard boxes, and other acidic materials. There are slide pages made out of acceptable plastics (polypropylene, polyethylene, and polyester or Mylar). Most slide pages are made with holes to fit a three-ring binder or take a hanging rod for hanging folders.

Slide boxes made of metal or polypropylene provide safe storage for slides as well. Some people like to store their slides right in the carousel trays. This is environmentally fine. The air circulation around each slide is actually good. It takes up much more space, however, than the other two methods.

Refrigeration of Photographic Materials

Often an environment combining low temperature with low humidity is hard to obtain. Refrigerating or freezing photographic materials in moisture-proof envelopes or cans is an excellent way to achieve these conditions. A word of caution, however: Before you start storing your photographic materials next to the ice cream, make sure you know what you are doing. Although freezers are cool, the humidity level in them is high— hence the need for moisture-proof containers. Disaster awaits if materials are put in the freezer in containers that are not made specifically for this type of storage.

Materials need to defrost in their original storage bags until all condensation has evaporated. Before doing this, make sure you read the instructions on the freezer sleeves or cans you purchase, so as to not harm your materials while trying to protect them. Black-and-white negatives should never be stored with color ones.

Damage Repair

Many valuable and priceless treasures have been lost to unfortunate disasters involving nature or human error. Preventing damage to valuables is always better than learning and employing restoration techniques. Practicing preventive maintenance by applying the information above will help. If you can, catch damage when it can be repaired simply. For example, support a small bend before it tears.

Unfortunately, there will be times when a disaster happens. It's good, when those times come, to know how to care for your photos. If there is *any* doubt in your mind as to what to do, do nothing. Stabilize the photo, then contact a conservator for instructions on how to care for your prints. A conservator or photographic professional will be able to make copies from slides, negatives, and prints that are damaged. A badly faded, stained, or cracked photo can be restored in a way that will sharpen and revive the image.

Fire. Fire is the most unfortunate disaster—once something has burned, there isn't much you can do to restore it. The best advice here is again prevention. Make sure you have good fire and smoke detectors. Keep copies or negatives of rare photos in a safety deposit box or at least in someone else's home.

Many people store valuable photos in a fireproof vault or box. Because extreme heat from a fire can damage photographic

124

materials, it's important to select a container carefully. Many specifications for fire files, safes, or boxes are for paper; photos are damaged much more easily. Many fire-resistant safes have a type of insulation that releases moisture when it is heated. The interior can also be filled with steam, which can damage photos. Purchase a vault that has enough insulation to provide good temperature control and prevent moisture condensation on the walls. Generally speaking, if the container prevents the temperature from rising above 100 degrees F., most materials will not be adversely affected. If temperatures exceed 150 degrees F., most photos will be damaged. Between those two temperatures, results will vary.

Water. One consequence frequently associated with a fire is the water damage inflicted when extinguishing the fire. Other sources of water damage are floods, burst pipes, backed-up sewers, and leaky roofs. Innocent squirt-gun fights have damaged some of my photos. Store photo albums or containers at least twelve inches above the floor to avoid water damage. Avoid storage in basements and attics, where leaks and water problems are more prevalent than normal living areas.

Wet photographic materials need immediate attention. Mold growth comes very quickly. Water softens the photographic emulsion and causes it to swell. Once the emulsion layer has softened, dirt can become lodged in it, causing distortion. If the print is wet for more than a few days, the emulsion will separate from the negative or print. Some of the dyes in color photos will disappear altogether.

Air drying is the best thing for wet photographic materials. Lay them out on a nylon screen if possible. This allows air to circulate all around them. A room where the temperature is below 65 degrees F. will help to inhibit fungal growth. Dehumidifiers and fans can help speed up the drying process. Never stack photos to dry. If they were stored in a stack, and the stack got wet, separate them before drying—but be careful: Sometimes even gentle pulling disturbs the emulsion. *Stop!* Don't continue pulling to try to separate them. Submerge the materials in cool, clean water, watching carefully to see that the emulsion doesn't dissolve. If the photos float apart, they may be air dried. If photos don't separate, remove them from the water and contact a conservator.

There are commercial photographic wetting agents on the market that can be used to rinse dirty slides. Slides should be dried upright, not flat. They can either be propped at an angle or hung on a line.

Tears, rips, and curls. Use archival tape to mend torn photos and negatives. Never put the tape on the emulsion side of photos or negatives. On a negative, it is hard to see which side has the emulsion. The emulsion side has a duller appearance than that of the shiny, nonemulsion side. (If you can find a scrap piece, you can lick it. The emulsion side will be stickier than the nonemulsion side.)

If a photo is badly curled from rolling, very fragile, or old, consult a conservator. If the curling is minimal, you can straighten it yourself. Purchase a pH-balanced sponge and blotter paper from a photographic supply store. Lightly wet the back side of the photo with the sponge. Put the photo between two sheets of blotter paper and place a heavy book on top for a few days.

Cleaning prints and negatives. There are photographic emulsion cleaners on the market that can easily remove most inks, finger oils, tape residues, mildew, smoke, and soot damage. Follow the instructions on the bottle carefully to avoid more damage, or allow a professional to help you. Never clean photographic materials that were made prior to 1900. Emulsion cleaners could destroy them.

Oldies

Few of us have ever seen a daguerreotype, ambrotype, or tintype photo, let alone owned one. If you are the lucky owner of such a thing, congratulations. Not only do you have a photo of someone who lived in the 1800s, you have a piece of history.

Daguerreotypes were introduced in 1839 by Louis Daguerre.

These prints can be identified by their copper base. The image developed in mercury vapor is very fragile. Their silvery, highly reflective finish makes the image hard to see in certain types of light. Never unseal the tape holding the copper plate and corner glass. Consult an expert.

An ambrotype was popular in the United States from 1854 to around 1870. They were invented by Frederick Archer, the inventor of the glass negative. These prints were made from a thin glass negative backed with black paper, varnish, or velvet.

Tintypes became popular in about 1860. This was a cheaper and more popular way to do photographs than the fragile glass ambrotype. Their base is a thin sheet of iron which has been given a coating of black lacquer. They have a very dull, muddy, greyish image.

Restoration of these old photos should be attempted only when the deterioration has proceeded so far as to totally ruin the existence of the image. Good quality copies should be made before starting any treatments. Because of the fragile and rare nature of these types of photos, consult a photo professional or conservationist for help. (The bibliography has some good book sources as well.) In the meantime, practice good environmental storage practices as mentioned throughout this chapter.

A Few Final Hints

For information on proper framing of photographs, see the section on framing in Chapter 9, "Keepsakes and Heirlooms."

For information about putting your photos on floppy and compact discs, or other computer storage and scanning devices, and about digital cameras, see Chapter 11, "Computers."

If you're looking for a great way to safely store an original photo and still have one to enjoy, consider photocopying. This is also a good way to get copies of photos that you don't own or have a negative for. Most large copy centers have the capability to make copies of photos that will look almost as good as the original. From a distance you really can't tell the difference. Color photos look good, but black-and-whites turn out the best.

I had some black-and-white copies made that we did a little light adjustment to, and they look *better* than the original.

When copying, use a high-quality, acid-free paper. This will ensure the longest life possible. Authorities have said they don't know of the long-term durability of copied images, but if done correctly they should last a very long time and not cause any harm to photos they come in contact with.

Only within the past 150 years have we been able to document history photographically. Think what history books would be like if we had photos of Christopher Columbus or the first Thanksgiving, and that will give you some idea of the historical value of photos. Photographs that record our memories deserve the same kind of care as any heirloom or valuable object. If we neglect to preserve our photographs, some of our history will fade away along with those images.

SCRAPBOOKS

"All that life is is the accumulation of memories."

LEO BUSCAGLIA

Certificates, cards, programs, newspaper clippings, receipts, announcements, invitations, résumés, licenses, ticket stubs, schoolwork, awards: this is the nostalgic "stuff" we keep to remind us of special places, people, and events. All these things and more can be stored in a scrapbook.

The worth of scrapbooks was brought home to me by a quotation from the Baroness Maria Von Trapp (the woman whose story was immortalized in *The Sound of Music*). In a speech given at Brigham Young University on November 18, 1965, she said: "My husband, belonging to the aristocracy and being an Imperial Navy officer, said, 'My family will never be on a stage!' (This was no prophecy.) He bought a scrapbook and he pasted in all these contracts which we got right after this, from all kinds of managers around Europe, from outside the 'Iron Curtain'—and one from America. We had the scrapbook for so many years. . . . All the time we sang to keep alive. We sang for just anything—for a hot meal, or for staying overnight, or for a birthday party, a wedding party, until we became known. Now we clutched to our hearts our most precious possession, the scrapbook." Their scrapbook had become the symbol of their prosperity, their talent, their ability to make a living. Scrapbooks can remind us of how wonderful our lives have been.

129

The Wrong Materials

If you want your scrapbook to last, not just any kind of book will do. Judith Fortson, the conservation officer at the Hoover Institution of Stanford University, says: "People think that by putting these family treasures in an album they're being preserved forever, to be passed down to future generations. Yet, in many cases, these albums are helping to speed their deterioration" (*New York Times*, October 3, 1987).

I have used many products for scrapbooks over the years that have ruined my photos and treasured memorabilia. I've tried almost every method you can imagine to make a scrapbook. About fifteen years ago I became terribly frustrated because most of them were falling apart:

1. Oily glues and tapes had soaked through and ruined papers and photos with a brown stain. Inks had bled and caused damage to some irreplaceable items.

2. Scrapbooks that I had assembled in report covers had cracked. Later I learned that the black construction paper used in the report covers is highly acidic and the covers are made of an acetate that is acidic. Besides, I had to three-hole-punch the papers that I inserted in them to get them to fit.

3. Bound scrapbooks were frustrating. Even books that used acid-free paper caused problems. I didn't like the fact that I *had* to mount the items I was saving. One side had to be glued down. Cards and items that had a front and a back couldn't have both sides viewed. And I now know that it's bad to have pages touch each other without a plastic covering or tissue between them to keep items from "kissing" each other. Photographs especially should never be placed where they will be right across and "kiss" each other when the pages close. Acids in them will migrate and the photos will scratch.

Another problem with bound books was that the pages had no protection against fingerprint damage and oils in my hands—a big cause of deterioration. These books didn't lie flat, and I never had anywhere to store them because a bound scrapbook tends to be larger than most standard bookshelves. This promoted deterioration because they were always getting kicked or knocked around.

4. Sticky or "magnetic" albums were causing problems too. The pages turned yellow and the cover sheets were ripping. Some of the sticky part was wearing off and things were just falling out. Other pages were so sticky that items wouldn't come off. (I found that by using a hair dryer to soften the glue, I could pull them out.) I also started noticing striped lines on my papers and photos as the oils from the glue on the pages were absorbed. These stains are permanent.

Another problem was that some of the glue from the sticky page transferred to the clear cover sheet. When I placed a photo, glue from the cover transferred to the front of the photo. When I tried to take the photo out, the front was glued to the plastic sheet and the back was glued to the sticky cardboard. The picture was ripped apart. I later learned that the cover sheets in "magnetic" albums are typically an acetate or polyvinyl chloride (PVC), which is highly acidic and chemically reacts with photos in a destructive way. Photos and other papers placed in the sheets are completely sealed in with the oily glue and the cardboard backing, which also is usually acidic.

Stay away from any of these types of materials for your scrapbooks! Sometimes the damage can't be seen for years, but once it happens it is usually irreversible. You should use only the best quality materials on your books if you intend them to last.

The Perfect Scrapbook

After all those years of bad experiences, I developed some criteria for what I would look for in the perfect scrapbook:

1. **Durable enough for anyone to look at.** Many people have baby books that are too fragile for their children to look at. I wanted to have books that could be enjoyed by everyone.

2. **Versatile and reversible.** I wanted to be able to take a photo out to use somewhere else, or to be able to read what was written on the back of a card. One year I was in charge of my

ward's Sweetheart Ball. We put red hearts on the wall and wedding photos of couples in the ward on the hearts. I was amazed at how many people couldn't get their photos out of their books. It was impossible to mount a bound scrapbook on the wall!

3. **Expandable.** I wanted to be able to match what I had started. Years ago I bought a scrapbook at a drugstore. When I was close to the end I wanted about five more pages. That store no longer sold that type of book or any refill pages for it. I wanted a system that I could keep going with and not be frustrated when trying to find matching pages.

4. **Reasonably priced.** I knew that if I started this project for my life, I couldn't afford to spend a fortune on it.

5. **Pretty and fun.** I wanted something that was nice looking, colorful, creative, and enjoyable to look at.

6. **Archival quality.** I wanted something that would last a minimum of 100 years. If I was going to go to the work to put something nice together, I wanted at least my grandchildren and perhaps their grandchildren to see it.

About this time, I started doing scrapbooks for the Church and ran across a great system that fits all the criteria that I wanted. It begins with polyethylene or polypropelene pocket sheet protectors. These are acid-free and will not lift print or discolor photos. They fit a standard three-ring binder and hold an 8½-by-11-inch piece of acid-free, buffered paper or card stock. Archival corner mounts, water-based glue with a neutral pH, or archival tape can be used to mount photos and mementoes. Permanent pens or colored pencils replace any markers that bleed or fade. For more details, refer to Chapter 2, "The Right Materials."

Here are some of the advantages to this system.

1. The advantage of a three-ring binder is obvious: Pages lie flat and can be added or removed at any time very easily. The size is easy for children to hold and look at. It also fits into my bookshelf.

2. The pockets are versatile. Items do not have to be mounted on a page. For example, all my report cards from

elementary school are loose in one pocket. They are not glued down, so I can pull them out and read each side of them.

3. Paper doesn't have to be used in the pocket. Cards can be opened up and laid flat to display both sides. I slipped in the guest pages from my wedding book, for example, and both sides of signatures can be viewed.

4. By using corner mounts or neutral glue, you can remove the photos when necessary.

5. Pretty colored paper can be used and you can mix and match as you please.

6. The pockets protect against fingerprints, dirt and smudges, oils in hands, and acid migration from one page to another. I never have to worry about anyone—even children—looking at my books.

7. Archival photo print protectors are available. These have individual pockets for photos and are made to fit all standard sizes of prints. They can be used alone or intermingled in a book with the regular-size pockets. You can write on the plastic with a photo marking pen to describe and date the photo. Some people even put stickers on the plastic sheets to liven them up.

8. Large-capacity pockets are also available that will fit thicker items such as comic books, magazines, catalogs, commencement programs, and even many junior high yearbooks. These fit right along in the three-ring binder with the other pages.

Cautions and Hints

Not all scrapbook pockets are acid-free. Some are made from polyvinyl chloride (PVC) or acetate. Check the box before you buy them to make certain they are polypropelene, polyethylene, or polyester (Mylar). These are safe to use. If the box doesn't specify this information, sometimes you can smell the bad ones. The vinyl type smell like new plastic toys or shower curtains to me. Archival pockets will have no smell.

Not all card stock or mounting paper is acid-free. Follow the guidelines in Chapter 2 to make sure that your paper is of good quality. Remember to get not just acid-free but alkaline-buffered paper. Use the good glues and pens described in that chapter as well.

You can purchase archival binders with slipcases to keep out dust; however, most scrapbooks for basic home use can be kept in any regular notebook for half the price of an archival one. Inexpensive barrier boards to protect the insides from binder acids can be added inside the front and back covers. If you are having problems with dust getting into the tops of the binders, you might try laying a fabric table-runner across the top of your shelved books. If you choose to use slipcases, you need to air out your scrapbooks once in a while. Often these cases are tight and don't allow necessary air circulation.

Make sure you write names and captions under photos and other memorabilia to identify them well. Tell stories about the items you are saving. The more you can write in your book about a photo or item, the better.

Write on the scrapbook page all the information about *who* is in the photo, *when* and *where* it was taken, and *what* the occasion was. Label the photo as well, just in case it ever gets lost from the page. (See pages 118–20 for hints on labeling photos.)

A reminder: Don't use glue or archival tape on fiber-based photos. These have a paper backing—although the adhesives are archival, they could rip the photo if it is taken off. For these types of photos, always use archival corners or cut slits in a sheet of paper and tuck the photo into them. A resin-coated photo has a shiny backside. Glues and tape come off of these photos easily. If glue ever sticks a bit, simply wet a cotton swab and gently push it under the photo to loosen the glue and ease the photo off the paper.

Getting Organized

One of the most important ways to speed up time and cut down on frustration in doing a scrapbook is to be organized. Many people don't start their scrapbooks because they are too overwhelmed at all the many boxes of "things" they have. They don't know where to begin. But once those things are organized, assembling a scrapbook is really not difficult at all.

There are many different ways you can organize your photos and mementoes. I like to place them chronologically; some people prefer to organize into themes or categories, such as holidays or vacations. (See "Types of Scrapbooks," below.) Either way is just fine. Here's what I did to organize my own materials:

I took apart all my old scrapbooks that were in bad shape. I got some acid-free file folders and labeled them with years. I then began to put everything I could find into the folders under the appropriate year. (These things included photos, certificates, letters, cards, programs, and other sentimental items that I had tucked into boxes or drawers.) Breaking it down into small, workable sections made the task much less overwhelming: Whenever I wanted to work on my scrapbook, all I had to do was pull out the next folder. I could place things chronologically into my book very easily. If you choose to do books in themes or categories, label your folders accordingly.

When I went to help my mother organize her things, it was clear that she didn't have as many items as I did. So we divided her folders into broader categories: her life before marriage, my dad's life before marriage, their New York years, 3rd Avenue years, and Wilton Way years. These divisions were sufficient to allow us to fit things chronologically into her books with no trouble.

Now that my books are caught up, my folders are labeled by months. For example, when I get film back from being developed, I put the photos straight into the folder showing the month they were taken. A letter, note, program, or article goes straight into the appropriate month's folder. I don't have to think about whether an item is good scrapbook material or not; I just simply put it in the folder. When I get that folder out to work on, I sometimes toss things away or put them somewhere else. The nice thing is that no matter how far behind I am in working on my scrapbooks, everything is organized all together and I can locate it at any time.

I have folders for my children and put many things straight into their folders. Double prints of photos can be made easily and shared between their folders and mine.

I am selective in the things I use in my books. I don't put everything in them. I have an acid-free box where I store "extras" and items I'm unsure about.

Types of Scrapbooks

Yearly or chronological. I like to do a family book each year. It's fun to look back and see all that we did in a particular year. I always include newspaper articles of the top stories of the year at the end. My yearly books go from January to December, but some people like to organize them by the school year, from September to August.

My children's books run in a straight chronological order until one volume is full. Some things are included in both their books and my own. For example, if Ceciley has a birthday party, she may have several pages devoted to it in her book. In the family book, we want to remember that she had a party, so I will put in one page of the day.

Themes. I have a festive scrapbook of Christmases that includes photos of my family from as far back as I could get until the present. This is in a beautiful Christmas binder and is a fun book to display during the season. You could include copies of family Christmas letters, special cards from others, or copies of letters sent to Santa. My family receives letters from Santa each year, so I keep those here as well. I also have a book of Thanksgiving photos from past years. I have a cabin scrapbook that shows the progress of the construction of our family cabin and has a list of guests that have visited there.

A "school book" is a fun type of theme album. I include class photos and a school picture, along with a photo of the child on the first and last days of a school year. Photos from class parties and field trips can also be included. I like to record the child's height, weight, teacher's name, and reminders of memorable events. My sister has a book with empty pockets; when the children bring home school papers to save, she quickly slips them into a pocket. Artwork that is too big to fit into a scrapbook can be reduced on a photocopier. You can take photos of projects such as salt-dough maps and volcanoes so that they can be remembered without cluttering up your closets. Make sure to include the artist child in the photo.

One of my favorite theme books is a birthday book. I like to have a nice portrait taken of each child on his or her birthday. If the child had a party, photos of that are included. Each year I fill out for the child a form that looks like this:

My Favorite Things

Date _____

Age _____

Height _____

Weight _____

Books _____

Colors _____

Songs _____

Movies _____

TV shows _____

Foods _____

Games _____

Toys _____

Sports _____

Places _____

Close friends _____

Hobbies _____

Favorite store _____

What I want to be when I grow up _____

I usually add a little bit about their personalities and exciting things that they are doing. It's fun to see how the entries on the form change from year to year.

Other theme books could feature vacations, weddings, family reunions, clubs, committees, friends, dating, sorority or fraternity, choir, or mission experiences.

137

Categories. A common way to organize a scrapbook is in sections or categories. These could include children, holidays, hobbies, school, career, church, vacations, friends, pets, civic activities, weddings, birthdays, and so on. This is like a theme book, but includes several categories in one binder.

Extended family book. Another wonderful type of scrapbook is the extended family book. I have a friend whose family has done a book like this for years. She has seven brothers and sisters, all married with families. Each individual family writes a summary of the year. Some do it in months; others do it with children's names as the headings. They are all different, but the year is highlighted and summarized in some fashion. The families also include pictures, articles, awards, and anything else significant for that year.

Each year they rotate the responsibility for the book. The person in charge makes copies of each family summary and puts them together to provide a complete family book for everyone.

Creative Ideas

There are so many things you can use to decorate your books. You can be as creative and individual as you want. Here are a few ideas to get you started:

Acid-free stationery can be used to frame photos or to back a narration.

Acid-free designer papers are available in many varieties on the market today. They remind me of fun wrapping papers. These are easy to use and make a page look great.

Stickers of archival quality add spark to a page.

Templates of all shapes can be used to trace around photos for cutting. This way you can fit more photos on a page and give them a special look. (I never worry about cutting a photo that I have a negative for. *I don't cut photos that I don't have negatives for.*) Templates or even cookie cutters can also be used to cut out colored paper for backgrounds. Note: Don't cut Polaroid prints. The alkaline developing gel can irritate your skin, and exposing the gel to the air may speed deterioration.

Colored pencils add brightness and are safe to use.

Borders and designs can be photocopied from clip-art books or made on a computer.

Fancy scissor cuts add flair to borders or photos. There are so many shapes and styles available. There are even scissors and corner rounders designed specifically to cut and trim corners.

Cropping photos down is perfectly all right. For example, excessive sky, water, mountains, or an ugly wall might all be cropped out to make a picture look better. However, some background things that seem mundane to us now may be fun to see years from now: old wallpaper before remodeling, the way the furniture was arranged, the knick-knacks in a room, the old fence or car. Think before you cut: some of what you see in the background can be nostalgic and might even help to date a photo.

Tracing around an item using a plain or fancy ruler adds a lot to a page.

Avoid Burnout

I have a dear friend who made a scrapbook for her first daughter. She spent countless hours putting together about a year's worth of material from her daughter's life. It is gorgeous and creative. However, she spent so much time, effort, and money on each page that she "burned out." She said: "Oh, Anita, I'm sick of doing scrapbooks. I've moved on to some other hobby." So, because she "burned out" on doing the one book, her second daughter will have nothing.

Often when I am giving presentations on scrapbooks, people feel overwhelmed and discouraged because they think they aren't creative enough. Some have seen cute pages that other people have done and feel that they don't have the time or energy to do their books that way. *You don't have to!* Please don't feel that your books have to be clever works of art. In fact, some of the nicest books I have seen are very plain and simple, with no added extras at all. They are very classy looking. *Remember, what you surround your keepsakes with is not nearly as important as what you are saving.* I have seen some books that were so fancy I wasn't sure what the mementoes were! Don't miss the point that you are saving memories and histories of lives to pass down to other generations. When a memento is overshadowed by decorations to the point that a person viewing the book is not focused on what is important, you have gone too far. Make your scrapbooks cute, creative, clever, and fun *if you want to and can.* But don't go overboard or have it become a burden, something that you won't want to continue through your life.

Storage

As with everything else made from paper, scrapbooks are adversely affected by strong light, high temperature and humidity, dust, dirt, and other pollutants. Since scrapbooks are mainly comprised of paper and photographs, you can review the guidelines in Chapters 2 and 7 to learn how to properly store your books. Always store your scrapbooks in a vertical, upright position. Stacking horizontally can cause abrasion and warping.

I have found many benefits from keeping scrapbooks. It's such a wonderful feeling to have my photos and mementoes saved in good condition and easily accessible. It's nice to have a visual life story to share with others. There have been countless times when I have turned to a scrapbook to verify or remember an event. (The more I have written about such events, the happier I have been years later.)

Perhaps my favorite benefit is what I see in my children. They love to look at their books. It's great to hear them exclaim proudly, "There's baby Joseph! There's Grandma! Look at Uncle George!" I love the sense of self-esteem they get from knowing that their lives are important and worth recording.

With a little attention to proper care and materials, you can create wonderful scrapbooks that will last a lifetime and beyond!

KEEPSAKES AND HEIRLOOMS

*Heirlooms speak to us of the past in a way
that nothing else can.*

Relics and keepsakes are an integral part of history. They share the past in a way that nothing else can. The most precious keepsakes in your family may have more sentimental than monetary value, but whatever the case, physical items that belonged to a relative and have been handed down from one generation to another are priceless to your family. These include anything from crocheted tablecloths, dolls, hats, quilts, paintings, books, embroidery, and candlesticks to furniture and clothes. This chapter will discuss ways to identify, enjoy, and care for these precious items. In all cases, use good judgment and common sense. If by chance you have a piece with historic significance or value, contact a conservator regarding your plans for cleaning and storage.

Inventory List

If I were to die and you came into my home to go through my keepsakes and other possessions, you would have no clue as to their sentimental value or meaning, *unless* you read my inventory list. Making a detailed heirloom inventory list is the first step in preserving these valuable treasures. Sentimentally valuable things might be forgotten without an identification or story written about them. Even my children and husband might forget all the details of each item if they were not recorded. An inventory list identifies items as special and prevents someone from unknowingly giving an heirloom to charity or a garage sale instead of to posterity.

An example of this is my mother's old, black, cast-iron roaster pan with lid. Growing up, I never thought twice about this pan she always used. One day she told me the wonderful story of how my grandfather carried that roaster pan from Germany by boat to America. Now that I know of its value to him and to my mom, the pan is very important and sentimental to me as well.

An inventory list isn't difficult to make. Simply walk through your home and go through your boxes of special things and identify them. Your list should contain:

1. A physical description of each item. For example, "White nylon blessing dress with pink rosebuds."

2. The name of the person to whom the item belonged. In the above example, my list then indicates that it was my blessing dress. If an item has been passed down, give as thorough a list as possible of all the owners.

3. List where, when, or from whom it came. Always keep track of your source in case you find conflicting information. I noted that my Aunt Lavena Turner made the blessing dress for me, and I included the date and place of my blessing.

4. Some of my items have a photo attached to the description to help with identification.

5. Some item descriptions have an appraisal of value included. If a professional appraisal has been made, attach a copy of this appraisal with its source and date to the inventory list.

6. Location of the heirloom is an important piece of information. Where is the item now? Is Grandma's quilt or rug at the cabin? Is the jewelry in a safety deposit box? Is your sister keeping the doll for a while? Obviously an item's location can change, so it's important to keep your list current.

7. To carry this further, it would be nice to write about why the item is special. This information could be attached to the

inventory list or possibly kept in your personal history category book.

I keep my inventory list in a fireproof box together with my will. This way it will more likely be found if something happens to me.

Labeling Relics and Heirlooms

Some people like to label relics, heirlooms, and keepsakes by identification numbers or names. These numbers can be recorded on your inventory list. Never use tape, pins, or paper clips to do this. Tape dries out and falls off, leaving behind a sticky residue that is hard to remove. When tape comes off, it can bring with it the fibers of textile or a piece of paint. Pins and thumbtacks can rust, causing harm to keepsakes. They also leave holes, which further weaken and damage the item.

There is a good way to mark keepsakes that are made of glass or metal: Find an inconspicuous spot on the item and wipe it clean. Paint a small area with clear nail polish (just big enough to write what you want). When the polish is dry, paint over it with white acrylic paint. Let this dry. Use a permanent ink pen and write the identifying information. Cover it with another coat of clear nail polish. Another option is an archival liquid for identification that can be purchased from an archival supply store (see appendix). This process is easily reversible.

Tags can also be tied around the artifact if you can be sure that they won't come off or get lost.

For labeling textiles, you can write on white cotton twill tape with a permanent laundry marker and then sew the label into a seam or tag. You want to put it in a place that is inconspicuous but easy to find. A ball-point needle is best because it does not make holes in the fabric; it forces the fibers apart so that the needle slips between them. Use cotton thread on cotton, linen, and unknown fabrics. Silk thread should be used on wool and silk.

My favorite way to identify a keepsake is to keep a photo of it with a story or identification of the item. These can then be catalogued with the inventory list or kept in a personal history.

Where to Keep Keepsakes

There are two philosophies about storing precious heir-looms. One choice is to keep them all in one box together. The advantage of this is that if you are ever faced with an emergency need to evacuate your home, you can grab your special box quickly. It is also convenient for locating them since they're all together. Steel cabinets or sturdy archival boxes can be used for this.

The second philosophy says, "Don't keep all your eggs in one basket." One woman told me that when she was remodeling her home she rounded up all her special, valuable things and put them together in boxes in one corner of her basement. She didn't want them hurt or damaged in the remodeling. One night the neighbors left their water running all night. It leaked through her basement window and destroyed nearly all her precious things! Usually a catastrophe such as a flood or fire doesn't completely destroy everything in a home. In such a case, if you had things in different areas of your home, chances are you wouldn't lose everything. Do what is best for you. If you do keep your heir-looms all together, just be cautious as to where you store them.

Being aware of where your keepsakes are is important. I once read a story of a man whose home was damaged by a raging flood. He had just a few minutes to gather any possessions he could before evacuating. He panicked under the pressure and grabbed his color TV. Later he realized that the TV was sitting on the old trunk that was full of family heirlooms. In an emergency situation we often aren't thinking very rationally. Be prepared. Know what and where your valuables are. You may own expen-sive furniture and appliances, but these can be replaced and are usually covered by insurance. Think about items that can't be replaced; make a list of them. Store these items near an exit or where you can have easy access to move them if necessary. I have two fireproof boxes that were not very expensive. I like them because they are small enough for me to carry, if needed, but hopefully also sturdy enough to withstand any natural disaster.

Obviously not everything can fit into them, but many things do. Of course, *no object,* however rare or valuable, is worth a risk to a person's safety.

Another solution to the storage of some of your valuables is to have copies made and stored in safety deposit boxes or at the home of a trusted family member or friend. Obviously, you can't photocopy Grandma's quilt, but you can keep photos and videos of physical items. Granted, they're not as good as having the original item, but they're immensely better than nothing.

Enjoy Your Keepsakes

One of the best things you can do with your heirlooms and keepsakes is to enjoy them. This can't be done if they are packed away somewhere. My mother has some beautiful crystal goblets that were given to her from her grandfather's estate. Two of them have been broken over the years. I guess if she had packed them carefully away and never used them, those two would never have been broken. But the family wouldn't have ever developed any memories of the goblets, either. When I see them in the china cabinet, I remember many Sunday, Thanksgiving, and Christmas dinners for which we used those goblets. On the other hand, I have a friend who has a set of beautiful sterling silverware. It is protected in her safety deposit box for fear she will lose or scratch a piece. Her family has never seen the set. They have no memories of Mom's silver. When she dies, it may have monetary worth, but no sentimental value. What are possessions for if we can't enjoy them?

I've heard many stories of people cleaning out homes of parents and grandparents and finding beautiful linens, stored away for years, that have been destroyed. If they had been used, they would not have sat folded for years, only to fall apart at the creases when found. Maybe they'd have a stain or two on them, but wouldn't that be better than having them fall apart with no memories at all attached to them? One grandmother stated, "Well, I was just waiting for a special occasion to use them." For goodness' sake, *have* a special occasion and use them!

Wedding dresses are no good boxed away forever. Get your dress out! Show it at Young Women Standards Nights; model it on your anniversary; find ways to share it. Why keep it if you never can enjoy it?

I met a woman who has her mother's graduation dress framed gorgeously on her stairwell wall. Next to it is a photo of her mother wearing the dress. Blessing dresses also look great in frames. Bonnets, spoons, tools, ribbons, medals, books, doilies, samplers, embroidery, handkerchiefs, watches, glasses, coins, jewelry, and countless other items of memorabilia can be framed and enjoyed.

My niece has a beautiful doll that is wearing her blessing dress. The doll sits in a darling little cradle to be enjoyed every day.

Care of Heirlooms

Although I feel strongly that we should enjoy our heirlooms, we should absolutely take proper steps to see that they are taken care of. Our valuables can last for generations if we take a little time and care. The following will discuss general care for valuables; then specific sections on different types of heirlooms will go into more detail about their unique characteristics. You will find, however, that the basics of light, humidity, and temperature control are common to most keepsakes.

Most damage to heirlooms and valuables comes from carelessness or improper storage environment. Understanding the effects of the environment and taking proper care can prevent minor damage and some major disasters. Some suggestions explained in this chapter are fairly easy, nontechnical procedures that anyone can do. Other methods are more complicated. Never attempt to do anything you don't quite understand. (I'll do my best at explaining!) It is often better to do nothing than to do something harmful or wrong. Don't be afraid to consult a conservator for help if you need it. You may avoid irreparable damage to a priceless antique.

Protect the integrity. I was reading in a doll magazine about

146

a doll that I've had since I was three years old. The monetary value attached to this old doll was astonishingly high. However, my talking doll is worth virtually nothing now—her insides were removed to be used in a brother's science project.

Before we cut up, throw away, or otherwise alter an item, we should think twice about it, and maybe even get a second opinion. What are we doing to the integrity of the item? Indeed, we cannot save *everything,* but be wise as to what you choose to alter or discard.

Gloves. Before caring for relics, wash your hands well and wear white cotton gloves. Your hands have a natural oil that transfers easily to any items you hold. Body oils can disfigure metal objects permanently; they also adhere to textiles very easily and quickly. However, never wear gloves when handling glass objects. These become slippery with gloves and you could drop them accidentally.

Temperature and humidity. Appropriate temperature and humidity levels are important. High humidity causes swelling in some items, promotes the growth of mold and mildew on most materials, and causes rust on metals. If humidity is too low, wood will split, veneer will pop off, paint may crack and peel, and paper will become dry and brittle. Generally, the ideal environment for most heirlooms is around 50 percent relative humidity and 68 degrees F. This is the best situation for a room containing varied heirlooms. For each individual case, read the specifics below.

Cycling. Fluctuations in the humidity level wreak havoc on most things. These fluctuations create expansion and contraction, causing wood to decay, paint to crack, and fibers in fabrics to age. It is crucial to store heirlooms in a climate that can be maintained at a constant level. Attics, garages, and basements don't allow for this; they are rarely at a constant temperature through the year. A hygrometer—a small instrument that measures humidity—can be purchased from a laboratory supply store. Once a balance is found, a humidifier or a dehumidifier can monitor the level. If you choose to use one of these machines, watch it closely, because dramatic changes in humidity are most damaging.

Light. All light, even low light levels, over an extended time can cause damage. Direct sunlight and the light cast by fluorescent light tubes contain ultraviolet and infrared rays. These cause wood to deteriorate. An example of this is my front door: There is a distinct difference between the wood that the sun has reached and the part that is shaded by the metal in the screen door. Light weakens paper. It fades photos, artwork, and inks. Light fades the dyes in fabric and weakens the fibers.

The easiest way to control sunlight is through the use of window blinds, drapes, shutters, or awnings. Fitting the interior sides of windows with an acrylic that absorbs ultraviolet light can provide additional protection. Two types are UF-3 Plexiglas™ and Acrylite OP-2. You can lessen damage caused by fluorescent light by either sleeving the tube in an ultraviolet filter or replacing the fixture with incandescent lighting. Incandescent lights, however, can cause heat damage if they are placed too close to an article. Simply speaking, be smart about where you keep your valuables. Never place them in direct light!

Natural Disasters

Once you have taken care of your heirlooms and valuables as well as you can, the next step is to guard against natural catastrophes. Disasters may include rain, wind, tornado, hurricane, dust storm, flood, earthquake, freezing precipitation, slow-rising water, and, in some areas of the world, volcanic eruption. Other disasters occur from mechanical hazards: structural collapse, explosion, fire, air-conditioning failure, heating failure, humidity-control failure, water-supply failure, sprinkler-system malfunction, electrical-power failure, extreme air pollution, fuel or chemical spills, and structural leaks. These two lists seem very ominous. If one of those disasters occurs, there may be nothing you can do. However, there are some precautions you can take to help avoid complete destruction.

148

1. Make a routine inspection of your home to identify existing hazards.

2. Install fire and smoke alarms. Keep fire extinguishers handy.

3. Exterior window shutters can be closed during storms and will protect from heavy wind and precipitation. Store valuables away from window areas.

4. Valuables should be kept well above floor level if floods are likely.

5. In earthquake-prone areas, breakables can be secured on display with specially constructed stands and supports, and large, top-heavy pieces of furniture can be secured to walls.

6. Keep important original documents, photos, and records in a safety deposit box or fireproof box.

7. Copies of valuable documents, photos, and records should be kept in another home, preferably in another area of the country.

8. Security alarm systems can protect against theft and vandalism.

Woods and Furniture

Light and temperature. In caring for heirloom furniture, follow the "Care of Heirlooms" precautions above for temperature and light. Strong light over a period of time is very hard on furniture. My friend received a beautiful, hundred-year-old couch from an aunt. The piece is in great condition except on the back where it was exposed to light through a window. The material there is faded and rotting.

Humidity. Both high and low humidity (above 70 percent or below 30 percent) can be damaging to furniture. Pieces that have inlaid, veneered, or painted surfaces are particularly susceptible. High humidity softens the adhesives that bind the inlay or veneer to the surface of the piece. High humidity also can encourage mold growth, corrode metallic parts, and cause a whitish finish to form if it penetrates the surface. If there is any fabric on the furniture, the humidity is hard on that as well.

149

On the other hand, low humidity causes materials to shrink (which can lead to cracking and splitting), joints to separate, pegs and screws to loosen, and adhesives to become brittle. Ideally, again, the temperature would be 68 degrees F., with a 50 percent level of relative humidity.

Mold. Mold indicates an environmental problem. This is probably due to a combination of high humidity, poor air circulation, and dust. If you notice mold on your furniture or smell mildew in the room, immediately lower the humidity, increase air circulation (ceiling fans are good), and locate the afflicted piece or pieces. Never use water to remove mold; it encourages and accelerates more growth. Brush off or vacuum the piece, and then treat it with an antimold agent. If there is a lot of mold, you may want to contact a conservator.

Dust. Frequent dusting (believe it or not) is one of the best things you can do to maintain furniture finishes such as high gloss, lacquer, or shellac. Dust is abrasive and damaging to finishes in humid weather because of its moisture-trapping ability. If you ever get a chance to look at a dust particle under a microscope, you'll see that it looks like a small boulder.

Marble should never be dusted or washed with any kind of cleaning detergent—the soil can become embedded in the porous stone. Vacuum marble with a brush attachment to remove surface dirt. Use a very diluted mixture of ammonia and distilled water—about ¼ cup ammonia to 5 cups water—to remove localized dirt. Don't rub the surface; gently lay a slightly dampened cotton wad over the stain. Follow this with a cloth slightly dampened with plain distilled water. Then use a soft, dry cloth to absorb the dampness.

Wax and oil. Paste wax, such as Butcher's Wax or Renaissance Wax, can be applied to pieces once every six months to two years, depending on how often the object is used. Carefully remove old wax with mineral spirits and cotton cloths to avoid wax buildup. Don't use liquid or aerosol spray waxes—they contain agents that can harm fine furniture finishes. Don't use water when cleaning furniture, because it will warp the wood.

Nondrying oils such as lemon, almond, olive, and mineral are not recommended for use on heirloom furniture with unfinished surfaces. The problem with these is that since oils do not dry, they attract dust. Applying oil to a waxed finish or wax to an oiled piece leaves the surface gummy.

Linseed oil and any products containing it should definitely be avoided for all wood pieces. It produces an irreversible chemical change upon oxidation. It darkens the piece and forms a surface that is tough and cannot be removed without damaging the finish.

Many conservators feel that stripping an original finish destroys the historical integrity of a piece. However, if a piece has been damaged by fire or water, there are exceptions to this rule. Treatment of severe damage should be entrusted to the care of a professional conservator.

Metals

Many of our heirlooms and keepsakes are made from some kind of metal. Candlesticks, trays, goblets, and pitchers have all been handed down from generation to generation. It's sad for me to see such beautiful pieces bearing dents and scratches due to negligence. Mother Nature is a culprit on her own, bringing corrosion—rust and tarnish—that can damage metals. Careful handling, cleaning, and storage can greatly minimize these problems and prolong the life of precious metals.

Rust. Rust can happen quickly and is hastened by salts in human perspiration, water, or air under certain atmospheric conditions. High humidity levels lead to rust. All metals benefit from low humidity, ideally below 35 percent with a maximum of 50 percent. When metal objects become wet, dry them as quickly as possible. Soft cloths, such as cotton diapers, can be used to wipe, and blow dryers can help with tiny crevices. (Do not use a dryer if the item has loose pieces.)

Rust can be removed by rubbing with a 4/0 steel wool. Be careful not to rub so much as to lose a design in the object. Residue from rust, dirt, and oils can be removed with alcohol or mineral spirits. After the rust has been removed, place the item in the sun until it is warm, then wax it with a microcrystalline wax such as Renaissance Wax. Strong acids and commercial rust removers should never be used on valuable objects. They can cause extensive pitting in the metals.

Tarnish. Tarnish comes from exposure to chlorides and sulphur in the air and water. Chlorine in water can cause problems on certain metals if left very long. Many foods and plants emit corrosive acids and fumes. Metal objects that come in contact with salt, sugar, vinegar, citrus fruits, nuts, vegetables, eggs, or other sulfur-containing foods must be cleaned thoroughly.

Copper, bronze, and brass all tarnish. Various additives are combined with copper to create alloys that have different properties. When tin is the major additive to copper, we get bronze. When zinc is the major additive, it is called brass. Copper and these alloys are very susceptible to corrosion. Fingerprints from bare hands on polished surfaces become etched in and are very difficult to remove. In most cases, it is aesthetically acceptable to let the natural patina or finish develop. Copper and its alloys should be stored in polyethylene bags, antitarnish papers, or silver cloth to minimize the tarnishing. Not only will this help them look better, but it will avoid unnecessary polishing.

Silver is another metal that tarnishes. More harm is done to silver by excessive or improper polishing to remove tarnish than by anything else. Beautiful surface details on silver have been lost forever simply from polishing. (Sometimes the patina caused by tarnishing is desirable to keep for aesthetic and protective reasons.) Even the finest polish is harsh and abrasive. The more you polish, the greater the tendency for scratching, and each cleaning removes a layer of this very soft metal.

Never use a commercial polish or cleaning compound when cleaning an heirloom. A calcium carbonate solution (precipitated chalk) may be purchased from a jewelry or scientific supply store. Polishing with this takes a little longer than with a commercial polish, but is far less damaging.

Polish should always be applied in a circular motion with a

152

clean cotton rag, diaper, cotton ball, or swab. (Be careful with swab sticks so you don't scratch the piece.) As soon as a piece of cotton is soiled, use another one. Corrosion on the rags can be abrasive to the metal. When you are finished, remove all traces of polish from the piece with a solution of distilled water (tap water may contain chlorine and sulfur) mixed with diluted Ivory or Orvus soap. Any polish left in the crevices can corrode and pit the metal. Following this careful cleaning, rinse the piece in distilled water and dry it immediately and thoroughly with a soft cloth or a hair dryer. Be very careful if there are other articles with the silver such as wood, bone, or ivory. These organic substances are highly susceptible to water damage and easily abraded by polish. Before cleaning, place plastic wraps over these areas to protect them.

If a silver piece is filled with plaster rather than pitch, do not immerse it in water. Consult a conservator for advice.

Some people like to use dipping solutions to get rid of tarnish, because they make it so easy. *Beware of them!* Potentially harmful acids in these solutions become trapped in crevices, hollow knobs, and handles. These acids will corrode the metal over time. Thiourea, an acid usually contained in dips, does not wash off thoroughly and needs to be removed from silver with an abrasive cleaner. Research has also concluded that thiourea is a suspected carcinogen. Dips remove *all* tarnish, even the desirable patina in engraved lines or recesses.

Electrolytic cleaning is *sometimes* recommended by conservators for removing corrosion. (Most still favor removing tarnish with a mild polish.) Use this procedure only if the piece is solid. A key ingredient to this solution is aluminum. Dissolve one ounce washing soda (sodium carbonate, soda ash) in one pint distilled water in a freshly polished aluminum pan. If a glass container is used, place several pieces of crumpled aluminum foil in the bottom. Immerse the silver item completely in the solution. Make sure that there is always at least one contact point between the silver and the aluminum. Pieces should then be washed in distilled water and dried thoroughly with a cotton diaper or cloth. Electrolytic cleaning is like dipping in that it will remove all tarnish.

Reversible resin or lacquers that coat and inhibit tarnish of silver are acceptable if applied by a professional. Improper coating can lead to severe corrosion problems. Use the coating only if the object is to be displayed and not used. If the coating becomes scratched, damaged, or yellowed, or if tarnish is showing through, the item should be recoated immediately. The newly exposed metal will corrode badly and may be impossible to clean.

Gold doesn't usually tarnish or rust, but it can easily become scratched and deformed. Gold can be washed safely with a neutral soap such as Orvus Paste and distilled water. Ethyl alcohol and a clean soft cloth can also be used. If your gold does corrode, contact a conservator.

Never use abrasive scouring pads of any kind on a metal object; they *will* cause irreparable damage. Buffing removes layers of metal and is not good. Replating after damage is done reduces the value of an object and results in a thick, undesirable coat that conceals the original surface detail.

Light and temperature aren't critical factors with metals. The only concern with temperature is that it often affects relative humidity. Cycling may cause metals to expand and contract, creating stress. The only potential harm from light would be the heat generated, which could possibly escalate the rate of tarnishing.

Glass and Ceramics

Fired ceramics and glass treasures are not affected by light, insects, humidity, or temperature. Most damage to these items comes from improper handling that leads to breaking. However, extremes or sudden changes in temperature can cause a piece to break or crack. (Did you ever put marbles in boiling water and then into ice water to see them crack?) Never place a cold plate in a hot oven, or a hot plate into the freezer.

Having taught pottery classes for quite a few years, I am well

154

aware of the characteristics of fired clay. Differences in the properties of high- and low-fired pieces, which give each their unique appeal, also necessitate differences in their care.

Cleaning of ceramics first depends on whether the object and its surface glaze are porous or nonporous. Ceramics that are high fired, such as stoneware and porcelain, as well as all glass, are nonporous. They can safely be hand washed in distilled water with a mild soap such as Ivory or Orvus. Never use ammonia, strong detergents, or scouring powder. *Never wash valuables in a dishwasher.* Chemicals in dishwashing detergent and the high heat may remove decorations such as gold rims or patterns. Fragile items in a dishwasher can also get jostled around by the water pressure and could chip or break. Use only lukewarm water for washing and rinsing. Hot water can cause certain glazes to crack or other fine glass to break.

Be careful to not let a wet object slip out of your hands. Always use your bare hands or latex gloves. Use both hands to support the object, never holding it by the spout or handle. Use a plastic dishpan inside your sink and very carefully turn and rotate one item at a time. If a glass object breaks, save every piece. Carefully place them in a padded container such as an egg carton. Contact a professional or conservator to repair the broken piece. He or she will know the best adhesive for that particular ceramic or glass.

Porous objects such as terra-cotta, earthenware, or unglazed Indian pottery have been low fired. Generally, decorative ceramic pieces made in a mold are also low fired. If completely glazed, such pieces can be wiped with a damp cloth. Partially glazed or unglazed pieces must be dry cleaned by a conservator. You can, however, remove dust yourself with a soft artist's brush. Sentimental or valuable unglazed pieces should never come in contact with water. You've probably seen stains and watermarks on terra-cotta pots that have had plants in them. These are hard to remove totally. Never place low-fired pieces in the freezer. Ice crystals can form in the body and expansion can cause cracking.

Books

Because books are made with paper, it is important to read the materials in Chapter 2 on dealing with paper, inks, and adhesives. The same care guidelines with regard to environmental conditions, damage control, cleaning, and storage apply to books. There are, however, some considerations that are specific to books.

First, books by their very nature contain causes of deterioration. Glues in many bindings attract insects and bugs that like to eat the pages and the binding. Little amounts of iron can be left in paper after manufacturing. These often react with a fungus and form brownish red spots called "foxing." These spots are almost impossible to remove. Cheap paper with a high acid content, like that usually used in mass-market paperbacks, results in dry, yellow, and brittle book pages. Sometimes acids left in leather bindings can cause them to disintegrate. Being aware of these problems can help you watch for signs of deterioration and take action before it is too late.

Storage. Books need to breathe. Good air circulation prevents spores and insects from making their homes in the books and causing damage. For this reason, tightly closed, glass-covered bookcases are not a good choice for book storage. Wrapping books in airtight plastics is harmful as well. These seal air out and moisture in. Wrapping in paper that is not acid-free also causes deterioration.

Metal shelves are preferable to wood due to the acids in wood. However, a wood shelf that has been painted with a water-based acrylic paint or lined with a piece of polyester (Mylar) is acceptable.

Make sure there is enough breathing room for each book you keep on a shelf. Keep one to two inches open on the top and back to allow air to flow. Books should be shelved closely enough to support one another but loosely enough that you could slip a pencil between them easily. Shelve books according to their size. This way they can support each other. If not supported, tall, limp books could become deformed. Large books should be shelved flat on the shelf with no more than three books stacked together. If the book is larger than the shelf, place a stiff, acid-free, buffered card under it to help support it. Sometimes it may be necessary to store large or thick books on their edges. If you do this, make sure you lay the book with the spine down and give adequate support to the covers so they don't spread out, expand, and deform.

To store and protect a valuable book the very best way, keep it in a custom-made box. (Make sure that acid-free, buffered board is used to make the box.) This type of box is often referred to as a "clamshell" box because it is hinged on one side and can open and close like a clam. Such a box will protect a book from light and dust and allow "breathing," but temperature and humidity must still be monitored. Use a box that fits the book exactly—otherwise it may "rock" around in the box and become deformed. If needed, add some crumpled acid-free tissue paper around the sides of the box to help with support.

A four-fold portfolio box can be used to accomplish the same thing as a storage box and is usually less expensive. Slipcases aid in protection, but the spine of the book will still be exposed to light. (Also, sometimes slipcases are hard to remove because they stick to certain cover materials.)

Original book jackets should be preserved. Polyester coverings can be made to help maintain the jacket. It may be best to keep the jacket off while using the book to keep it in good condition.

Many people tuck newspaper clippings, old letters, or notes between the pages of books. In as short a time as a few months, discoloration from the clippings or letters can occur on the book pages. If you need to store clippings or notes in a book, keep them between sheets of acid-free tissue paper, deacidify them, or put them in a book that is not at all precious to you.

I have used books many times to press flowers and leaves. I'm sure I'm not alone in this practice, but it's not a very nice thing to do to a book. Not only does it cause indentations to the pages from pressure and moisture, but it stains the pages as well. There are better things to use in pressing flowers, such as a flower press! However, if you have no other resource and need to do it, please use a book that holds no sentimental or monetary value, and place the flower between two sheets of wax paper.

Handling. When taking a book out of a shelf, never pull it by the headband, which is the weakest part of the spine. Doing this can cause damage to the spine and eventually rip the headband right off. The correct way is to grasp the book in the center of the spine. If possible, reach to the back of the shelf and push forward from the open or fore edge. Place large or heavy books on a table before opening them. Support from another book or object may be needed to rest the cover on so the binding is not stressed from lying flat.

Use flat, acid-free bookmarks to hold your place. Paper clips, pencils, and similar objects can cause damage. Folding down the corner to mark your place is obviously damaging to the page. Leaving a book open flat or placing it face down can cause damage to the spine of the book. Use a bookmark and close the book when you're finished.

Never mend a tear or rip with anything other than an archival quality document- or book-repair tape. For books with great value, it is worth using a conservation method with Japanese paper and paste. Consult an expert conservator.

Cleaning. All bookshelves should periodically be emptied and cleaned. Books should be dusted with a soft brush and inspected for signs of mildew or insects. Light vacuuming can be done as well. Cover the hose with a piece of cheesecloth and use a low setting. Wash and dry the shelves thoroughly before replacing the books. If any book has signs of insects or mildew, isolate it so the book doesn't infect others. Consult a conservator for treatment of the infected book.

You can clean up some stray pencil marks and surface dirt yourself. Use a soft vinyl eraser or erasure crumbs from a vinyl eraser.

Rebinding. Rebinding a book that is falling apart will help it last longer. But before you rebind any book, consider the value and rarity of it. In some cases, rebinding will lower the value of the book. The closer a book is to its original condition, the more it is worth.

Book-shaped boxes can be made to store a worn book. These contain a spine label, look like a regular book, and can be stored on the shelf like an average book. You can make these yourself or purchase them through an archival company (see appendix).

An easy way to keep a worn, loose book together is simply to tie it together with flat cotton tape. Make sure it is tied at the open, fore edge of the book.

Textiles

A lot of keepsakes and heirlooms we collect are textiles, or fabric. These cover a wide range of materials: natural plant fibers, such as cotton and linen; fibers from animals, such as silk, wool, fur, leather, and feathers; and man-made synthetic materials, such as nylon, polyester, rayon, and acetate. Clothing can have sentimental value due to the event surrounding the wearing of an article, such as a graduation, wedding, or blessing dress. People also feel sentimental toward everyday pieces that simply were worn a lot, from Daddy's favorite tie to Grandma's apron. Feelings and emotions are also evoked when we see a child's baseball cap or first blanket.

Textiles and their stories are great ways to preserve and share history. I had a very spiritual experience when I was looking at the clothes Hyrum Smith was wearing when he was shot at Carthage Jail. Although our clothing may not promote quite that profound an experience, it will be valuable to our posterity.

Often, in the name of preservation, people accidentally harm articles more than if they had just left them alone. Textiles and fabrics of all kinds can be enjoyed a long time if cared for correctly. When they are mistreated, they can disintegrate very quickly.

Many things can promote the deterioration process. Common culprits are light, acidity, temperature and humidity fluctuations, insect and fungal attack, dust, acidic wood, paper and plastics, tight folds, perspiration, natural body oils, and food and protein stains. Problems also come from simple lack of adequate support when an article is moved or hung.

Light. Textiles, like other keepsakes talked about in this chapter, are very susceptible to light. Colors and dyes fade and yellow, fibers become brittle and weak under sunlight and strong artificial light. Both of these contain a high percentage of ultraviolet radiation. Keep shutters, drapes, and blinds closed when the light from the sun is the brightest. UV filters can be used over fluorescent lights to block damaging light rays. When photographing heirloom textiles, never use a flash. One flash is equal to eight hours of direct sunlight.

Temperature and humidity. Ideal storage for textiles is a dark, cool, dry place where air can circulate around and through them. A temperature of 55 to 70 degrees F. and a relative humidity of 40 to 50 percent is good. Textile fibers, especially those from animals and plants, absorb water quickly and easily from humidity. This water can cause the fabric to lose its shape and strength and can leave stains. Too much humidity can also cause mold and mildew. Warm temperatures and high humidity are excellent breeding grounds for insects. Wool and silk are especially prone to attracting moths and carpet beetles.

Too dry an environment is not good either. This can cause fibers to become brittle. Fluctuations (cycling) in temperature and humidity are particularly hard on textiles. Fibers will expand and contract with the temperature, causing them to weaken. Store all heirloom pieces at an appropriate, constant level.

Pollution. Any kind of smoke or exhaust is damaging to textiles. Airborne dust and dirt easily work their way into the fibers of the material. This is especially true if there is any kind of humidity fluctuation. The dirt settles in while the fibers expand and contract. Dirt and dust are very gritty and can actually cut into the fibers.

Inherent problems. There are also built-in enemies to textiles, problems associated with the actual materials or makeup of

160

a given textile or article. In the past, iron was often used in black and brown dyes. This iron literally eats the fabric away over time. Some early chemical dyes bleed even when slightly damp. This made wearing, and now cleaning, of these fabrics very difficult. Some silks had metallic salts added, which now are causing the fabric to crack. All of these inherent problems are virtually irreversible and there is nothing you can do. A conservator may be able to help you stabilize the article, however.

Handling and labeling. Before handling a vintage article, it is best to wash your hands well. It's also a good idea to wear white cotton gloves to keep oils from your hands from being transferred to the fabric. Be aware of any jewelry you are wearing, especially rings and watches, that could catch and snag the article. Of course, choose a clean working area. I like to put a clean, fitted sheet on my kitchen table. Keep food and drink away; accidents happen too easily.

Never write on the fabric with ink. Cotton twill tape can be written on with a laundry marker to identify the piece. Carefully hand stitch this with cotton thread to the garment tag, seam, or muslin bag you plan to use for storage of the item. Labeling a storage box with a permanent pen is another suitable option.

Recording information. It is important for your heirloom textiles to be identified. Describe the articles, where they came from, and, if they are clothing articles, who wore them. This information adds to the value of the piece. If possible, keep these identifications in the bag or box with the article. Always record the source of your information as well. This will aid if you ever come across conflicting information. (See information on inventory lists at the beginning of this chapter.)

Damage repair. Before cleaning a period piece, look closely for thin, worn spots, rips, holes, loose snaps or buttons, broken zippers, or other signs of damage. Thin spots are often found around folds such as pleats and tucks. Fibers become brittle and thin with age and light exposure. They will break along folds first, where they receive the most stress and abrasion. Carefully reinforce the tears and thin spots with netting. Moiré net is a fine, lightweight net used often to make bridal veils. It is less obtrusive than many kinds of netting, but strong enough for reinforcement.

Hand stitch the netting to the fabric with a cotton thread if the piece is cotton or if the fabric is unknown. If you know the fabric content, sew with matching thread (polyester, silk, wool). Use a small embroidery needle; it has a ball point and will not damage the fibers quite like a sharp-pointed one will. (With some extra-fine fabrics, however, a fine, thin, sharp needle could be best.) Use only a single thread and no knots. Sometimes a thread from the fabric has become unraveled but is still attached—if it is long enough, your best choice is to use this thread. I have had this happen a lot with knitted sweaters. Replace broken or rusted zippers, snaps, or buttons.

When you assess and repair damage and weaknesses in textiles, it helps to use a magnifying glass. You can purchase a good magnifying glass designed for seamstresses from a quilt or craft store. This rests on your chest, leaving your hands free, and will help you see the warp and weft in the weave as you stitch.

If your piece is fragile and in really bad shape, with big holes, repair may be impossible. The best thing to do is to stabilize it the best you can. Check with a museum supply shop and purchase a very fine net fabric that can be sewn over badly worn spots to hold things in place without further damage occurring.

If your valuable textiles have suffered from water damage or mud, they are subject to growth of mold and mildew. This happens really quickly. If the fragile fabric has survived the water without shrinking or without its colors running, it can be gently washed. Do this as soon as you can—before the fabric dries, if possible. If the damage is extreme or the fibers are delicate, weak, or brittle, a textile conservator should be consulted. If the fabric is wet and cleaning can't be done quickly, wrap it loosely and gently in an airtight plastic bag (the only time you should put it in this type of bag!) and put it in your freezer until you can take it to a conservator. Freezing puts the article in a state of limbo

162

and keeps the mold from spreading. It also prevents some stains from setting and stabilizes bleeding dyes.

Cleaning Textiles

Any kind of soil, whether it be dirt, perspiration, or food, should be removed before a textile item is stored. These spots can eventually eat the fibers and cause rust or mildew and rotting. Food stains are fertile ground for insects and fungus. Food and perspiration may be invisible at first, but they become evident over time. Usually fabrics can handle some kind of cleaning without much problem. In fact, Colleen Gregory, who owns City Cleaners in Salt Lake City (a good conservation cleaner), says that some old materials are much better than the new fabrics she sees.

Yellowing can occur on fabrics from aging or chemical reactions due to storage in wood or plastics. Cleaning may take out some of the yellow—however, don't be discouraged if a little bit stays. Some yellowing and age spots should be thought of as part of the history of the item. I think these marks of age often give the articles more character.

Vacuuming. Many museum conservators feel that vacuuming is the first choice in cleaning textiles. When *dry* fabrics have deposits of loose dirt and dust, a thorough, gentle vacuuming is very good. For valuable old quilts and rugs that are heavy or large, this is probably the only way to clean them.

Secure a fine polyester screen or nylon mesh over the nozzle of the vacuum, or lay a fiberglass window screen carefully over the piece. Make sure the edges of the screen aren't "raw." These raw and frayed edges can badly snag an article. If you need to, cover the edges with cotton bias or twill tape. A low-powered or hand-held vacuum is best. Vacuum on the lowest setting and open the vent if there is one. This will remove dust and dirt without stressing the fabric. Vacuum slowly and systematically, never just scrubbing back and forth. It is best to vacuum both sides of the article. Some conservators vacuum textile articles every six months as a regular maintenance routine.

Airing. Sometimes antique, vintage pieces are so deteriorated that I don't recommend any form of cleaning, but instead suggest airing. Something this fragile should never be hung; that adds stress to the fabric. Gently lay the article over a chair, sandwiching it between two cotton sheets. If weather permits, take it outside, preferably on a day or evening that is shady and breezy. (But don't let your articles blow away!) I like using my trampoline to lay the article on because air circulates well through it, but any table will do, or even the ground. However, if you put something on the ground, lay the sheet on several blankets so moisture from the ground won't come through. Airing for several hours is usually long enough. Keep a close watch to avoid harm from animals, weather, or other factors. I have aired fabrics inside by an open door or window and received almost the same effect.

Never air an heirloom article that is wet. Dust and fungal spores are attracted to the wet fabric and will stay on the textile after it is dry. These can cause further deterioration.

Dry cleaning by a skilled professional. If the fabric is wool, silk, or an unknown, it should be professionally dry cleaned by hand. If any perfumes, deodorants, or other soils are on the fabric, this cleaning should help to neutralize them. *Always patronize a cleaning establishment with a professional on the staff who is trained in conservation care.* Choose one carefully and don't be afraid to ask a lot of questions about how they handle old clothing.

The right type of dry cleaner will use a Stoddard Solvent that is petroleum based, not a synthetic-based chemical. Antique clothing should be cleaned alone with fresh solvent. A normal piece of clothing may be cleaned for thirty minutes; with an heirloom piece, possibly only a five-minute cleaning would be advisable.

Wet cleaning. If a fabric is man-made, cotton, or linen and *not too deteriorated*, you can easily clean it yourself. Always hand wash the articles; *never use a washing machine.* The agitation of the machine can literally tear a piece apart.

First check the dyes for colorfastness by saturating a small area of the piece with distilled water. Blot it with a clean, absorbent paper or cotton ball. If the color from the dye appears on the blotter, do not wash the textile in water. It will bleed or "crock." A textile that bleeds will have to be dry cleaned. If no dye appears, do the same test again, this time mixing a small amount of Orvus or a flake detergent in with the distilled water. (Orvus is a very mild, nonionic detergent. It reduces and neutralizes the pH to almost zero. Quilting stores and veterinary supply stores carry it. A solution of Lux or Ivory flakes with a bit of washing soda and distilled water can also be used.) If nothing happens this time, go ahead and wash. Never use commercial laundry detergents or bleaches for old or fragile fabrics; they are too harsh and will deposit damaging substances in the fibers.

Make a support screen with a length of polyester, fiberglass, or nylon screen. Attach PVC pipe to each side of the screen by sewing a casing for it around the edges. (I've even just used duct tape to attach the pipe. The idea is to give the screen a little more stability and allow you to lift it easily.) The reason for the screen is that fabric becomes very heavy and weak when wet and may need support to hold its weight. You don't want to stretch or rip the material or cause any added strain when lifting it from the water. Fill a tub or a small, clean wading pool with distilled water (anywhere between 50 and 90 degrees F.; never use hot water) and the appropriate amount of Orvus (follow the recommendations on the product box). Don't use too much soap; it will make rinsing difficult.

Soak the article on the support screen for half an hour at room temperature. If it is heavily soiled, you can gently agitate it with the palms of your hands. Do not use your fingertips—they exert too much localized force. Old fabrics become weaker in water and can easily be torn. Never wring, twist, or squeeze the article. Empty the soapy water from the tub and rinse the item several times in distilled water to make sure there is no soap residue.

To dry the piece, place the screen with the article on it between two undyed terry-cloth towels and pat out the excess water. Use your hands to gently straighten the wrinkles. Allow the article to dry thoroughly—a minimum of twenty-four hours in a dry climate—before storing it. Never dry heirloom textiles outside. Dust particles and fungal spores are attracted to wet fabric. These will remain on the textile after drying and might cause further deterioration. Also, outside you have the problem of exposure to sunlight and its harmful ultraviolet rays.

When washing a badly deteriorated textile, take much more caution. Sew the article between two pieces of thin gauze fabric. (Do not sew on the article itself, but rather make a bag for it.) Place the gauze-encased article on the screen and lower it carefully into the water. Use the palm of your hand to gently press the article under the water and then don't touch it again. Agitate the water around the sides of the screen. Rinse at least three times to remove the soap. Dry the article by allowing it to drain onto dry towels.

Dyes tend to run most when an article is drying, not when it is being washed. To prevent this, don't let your item drip dry. Immediately press the article between towels after the last rinsing. Carefully use a hair dryer on a warm setting to quickly dry it. This technique is obviously more effective on small items such as a sampler than on larger items such as a quilt—just do the best you can.

Hints. Avoid ironing, if possible. If it absolutely needs to be done, press the article inside out with a cool iron and place a cheesecloth between the article and the iron. Steam can be used for cotton and linen. If the item is large and fragile, it should be supported while ironing. For example, lay the skirt of a dress on a chair or table by the ironing board while ironing the bodice. Never iron fabrics with a "pile" such as velvet or corduroy, because you will crush the fabric and leave a sheen.

Never starch heirlooms. It is very harmful to textiles. Starch attracts silverfish and other insects for its food value, and it also causes the fabric to become increasingly brittle with age. If fabrics already have starch on them, it should be removed. An enzyme treatment is needed for this and a conservator must do it for you.

Rest textiles on a clean table (preferably covered) when working with them to avoid putting undue stress on the fibers. Never shake the item to remove the folds or to freshen—this also puts added stress on seams and fibers.

When in doubt about anything, *call a conservator!*

Storing Textiles

Three of the most common mistakes that I have seen made in storage of textiles are: no protection, folding, and storage in plastic. These are all big no-no's!

Rule 1: Have respect for heirloom pieces and protect them. Too many priceless pieces turn into kids' play costumes. One day while visiting a friend, I noticed her four-year-old daughter running around in her great-grandmother's wedding gown. The bottom of the dress had been completely cut off to fit the child better! Many a valuable piece of clothing is ruined when a person larger than the article tries it on or wears it. Seams can only take so much tension before they fray or rip. Many old things make great costumes, but keep important heirlooms out of the dress-up box.

Rule 2: Heirloom-quality pieces should never be folded. Fibers get an extra stretch around a fold. Where the folds and creases are, the fabric fibers bend and become weak, eventually tearing. Another problem with folding is staining. I once laid out a beautiful white tablecloth that had been stored for a while, only to find that brown stripes had stained the cloth all along the fold lines. A dark tablecloth will discolor and fade on the folds.

So if you can't fold a cloth item, what *can* you do? Here are three options:

Flat storage—my first choice. The best thing to do with fabrics is to store them flat. When a textile is resting flat, there is no tension or stretch pulling on the fibers. A good place to store a quilt is on a bed that isn't used much or doesn't get much light. Rotate it seasonally to avoid any fading. Flat storage also works well with handkerchiefs, doilies, and other small items. However, if you are like me, you don't have a lot of storage space on extra beds where you can lay wedding dresses, linens, and quilts out flat. Sturdy, durable, acid-free storage boxes can be used to store these larger items. (Remember that regular cardboard boxes and paper bags are acidic.)

The size of most garments and articles to be boxed is usually greater than the size of the archival storage box. Most textile or garment boxes have dimensions of about eighteen by thirty inches and are six inches deep. If your items don't fit flat, they should be "rolded," a coined term referring to the method of folding an article by using rolls. You never want to crease a fabric, so, wherever you would fold it to fit in the box, make a gentle roll, a fat fold—in other words, "rold" it. You can make "snakes" of cotton muslin or acid-free tissue paper to place in the "rolds," assuring that they will not flatten out. You should also place acid-free tissue paper between the layers of the fabric so that the fibers don't rub and wear against each other. Crumple acid-free tissue and stuff the bodice and arms of a garment to help hold its shape. If you're storing a wedding dress or uniform, it's nice to attach a photo of the person wearing it to the box.

Be cautious of archival boxes with little windows on the top. These were made so that you could see what is inside. However, light will go into the box where the hole is and can fade just that one spot of the fabric. I'm also a little leary of companies that seal your dress in an airtight box. Remember, fabrics need to breathe. Also, if your dress is in a sealed box that you can't open, how can you enjoy it?

Rolled storage—my second choice. Rolling is good for tablecloths, linens, rugs, shawls, or quilts. You can purchase archival tubes or treat large cardboard tubes with a deacidification spray. They can also be covered with Mylar to prevent acids from migrating.

Acquire a tube that is at least four inches wider than the article being rolled. Roll a piece of muslin or acid-free tissue around the tube as a starter; then begin rolling with your article on a flap of the starter. Interleave tissue as you roll to keep fabric from rubbing against itself. Roll with the front side of the textile away from the tube: with articles that have a lining, this will cause the lining to take the wrinkles. With carpets and other textiles that have a pile, roll in the direction of the pile, face out. Once it is rolled, wrap the fabric with one last piece of tissue; then wrap a piece of 100 percent cotton muslin (prewashed to remove sizing) around the article as a cover. Tie the ends with cotton strips or tuck the muslin ends into the roll. You may wish to tie some strips in the middle of the tube, depending on how long it is. My mom stores her table linens this way and hides them behind the couch.

Sometimes a piece is too large to fit a tube, or space for storage of a long tube isn't available. "Rold" the article into thirds and then loosely roll it like you would a sleeping bag. Make sure to use the cotton snakes or acid-free tissue to keeps the "rolds" from creasing. Once or twice a year, refold your article, putting the "rolds" in a different spot. Prewashed cotton muslin duffle bags can be made to store bulky items as well.

Hanging storage—my least favorite, but sometimes necessary. Another way to store an article without folding is to hang it. This may be necessary with fabrics with a nap such as velvet, corduroy, or furs. It is not my first choice because some articles, such as a wedding dress, may be very long, heavy, and bulky. (My friend's has a fourteen-foot train!) A heavy piece of clothing may be pulled and stressed at the shoulders or waist. I've seen beautiful old dresses that were in great condition except at the shoulders where they rested on the hanger. The fabric had worn thin and was rotting there.

To avoid that problem somewhat, never use wire hangers for hanging old garments. They are subject to rust, which can transfer to the fabric or the garment. They are also thin and give no support to the shoulders. A trick I learned from the Daughters of Utah Pioneers is to use a padded wooden hanger. This can help to alleviate some problems in hanging by padding the shoulder area and widening the support.

Make sure that the wooden hanger used has been painted with a water-based, clear acrylic paint. This will protect your garments from the tannic acid and formaldehyde found in the wood. A long shank on the hanger helps alleviate creasing of stand-up collars; it's also nice if the hanger has a bar across the bottom for extra support. You can wrap quilt batting in strips around the hanger, topping with a layer of cotton muslin to hold the batting in place. Even better is a sewn muslin cover that can easily be removed for cleaning.

Try to create a hanger that feels like a shoulder. (Have you ever pulled a sweater out of the closet and found the shoulder misshapen from the points on the hanger? This is what you are avoiding with the padded hanger.) The hanger should be padded according to the weight of the garment to be hung—if the hanger is for a coat, it should be more heavily padded than one used for a cotton dress.

Store the article in a garment bag made from prewashed, unbleached, 100 percent cotton muslin, which you can purchase from any fabric or quilt store. It's not necessary or even advisable to use snaps or zippers on the bag. Although most snaps and zippers are coated, I have seen some rust in humid climates. There's also a hazard with the potential for catching a garment in a zipper. Sew your bag with a casing at the top and use a cotton drawstring to pull it closed and tie it around the hanger.

Crumple acid-free tissue paper to stuff in and around the sleeves, bodice, and other places to help the article hold its shape. If you are storing a long dress, roll the bottom of it as described in "rolled storage," above, to fit in the bag. Some of the "deadweight" hang can be eliminated by taking pressure off the shoulders of the hanging article. Attach some strips of material to the bottom of the bag and tie them around the top of the hanger. Or gently rest the bottom of the bag on a stool or box inside the closet. You don't want it "scrunched up"—just gently resting to take pressure off the hanger.

Another way to take pressure off a dress with a heavy skirt is to make suspenders for it. This is also the way to hang a skirt.

170

Baste cotton twill tape to the waistband with a ball-point needle. Sew additional cotton strips onto the waistband tape in the front and back to look like suspenders. The suspenders are placed over the padded hanger to help reduce the pull of gravity. When helping to take pressure off a heavy dress, pull the suspenders a bit tighter to take up some of the weight. These sewn-in suspenders should be used with any large or heavy articles you wish to hang.

When using the hanging method, remember to give the article a rest periodically. Lay it out flat on a bed when you go on a vacation, for example.

Rule 3: Never store fabric items in a plastic wrap or garment bag. Textiles need to breathe. Plastic bags do not allow this to happen. They stop air circulation and trap moisture. Bill Ormond, curator of collections at Pioneer Trail State Park, says that a 100 percent cotton muslin bag (as described above) is a thousand times better than a plastic bag! Have you ever seen a sandwich or bread bag with water condensation in it? Well, you don't want the same thing happening in your garment bag. Some bags also contain PVC, which breaks down fibers. Storage in plastic bags causes discoloration, yellowing, and chemical reactions that bring about rotting. Plastic bags from the cleaners are often printed—those inks can rub off. Don't use them! The cleaners supply them only to act as a protection while you travel home, not for any extended storage.

Your regular living areas are the best places to store fabrics. I have never had clothes fall apart and rot when they were hanging in my bedroom closet. Sometimes people get really stressed about a sentimental piece and fold it up, pack it tightly in a plastic or paper bag, and put it in a box in the basement to be "safe." It would be much better to just let it hang in your closet!

It is a good idea to wash your cotton bags and muslin hanger covers twice a year. The best way to do this is with Orvus soap or Lux or Ivory flakes. Acid-free tissue paper should also be replaced once a year.

Cedar chests have the reputation of being the Cadillac of storage products for clothing and other textiles. They are not!

They do protect against moths, light, dust, and other critters. But the tannic acid and formaldehyde found in most woods, including cedar, cause deterioration and discoloration of fabrics. I have also seen oily spots on fabrics from where the cedar has "bled" sap onto them. If you still choose to put fabrics in cedar chests, keep them in cotton pillowcases, sheets, or unbleached muslin, and lay them on a piece of acid-free plastic such as Mylar. Articles that have been stored properly in boxes, as mentioned above, can also be placed in the chest. Wash the coverings twice a year, as mentioned above. Keep the articles away from the sides or unprotected bottom of the chest to prevent the cedar from "bleeding" onto the article and acids from the wood from migrating to the fabrics. The same conditions and precautions are true for cedar closets. Keep the articles away from the walls.

If you need to keep your linens in wooden drawers, line the bottom of the drawers with Mylar or acid-free cardboard, or seal them with a water-based acrylic paint or water-borne polyurethene varnish. Glad Bags are also nonacidic and can be used to line a drawer or shelf. Hard woods are better than soft; they have fewer wood by-products. But even though wood can be protected, it's best to find another alternative. Closets with wire shelves provide good air circulation. Rust-free metal shelves are better than wooden drawers or shelves as storage places for boxes or bags containing textiles.

I don't recommend the use of mothballs. They cause problems if they come in contact with fabric.

Selecting tissue and boxes for storage. Textiles made from plant fibers, such as cotton, linen, flax, and jute, are composed of cellulose and are easily deteriorated by acids. Acid-free, *buffered* tissue and boxes have an alkaline reserve to neutralize acids and are good to store these types of fabrics in. Textiles made from animal fibers, such as wool and silk, are composed of proteins. These are deteriorated by strong alkalis. These textiles should be stored in acid-free, *unbuffered* tissue and boxes.

For textiles that have both plant and animal fibers combined, or if you are unsure of the fabric content, use an unbuffered tissue or box. Remember that acid-free boxes and tissue that are unbuffered may in time turn acidic from migration of materials they come in contact with. It is good practice to test the acidity level yearly with a pH testing pen (see Chapter 2). If they come out acidic on the test, get new tissues or boxes. You may want to check your buffered materials as well—however, the buffering agent should prevent migration of acids to the tissue or box.

Leather

Treatments for leather vary, depending on the type of processing used in tanning the leather. Take any valuables to a leather tanner and ask advice before you try anything yourself.

Cleaning leather with water can be worse for the object than leaving it alone. The only safe thing for an untrained person to do is wipe with a soft cloth or vacuum.

Framing Artwork, Certificates, and Heirlooms

Framing your artworks, certificates, and heirlooms is a good way to enjoy and display them. If done properly, framing is also a good way to store articles. Many things have been ruined, however, by improper framing. Framers in the past were not always aware of conservation methods; museum-quality standards and the use of archival materials are relatively new.

Valuable artwork and photos need to be protected from framing materials that are harmful. Be sure that the framer you choose is familiar with museum-quality standards. Don't be afraid to ask a lot of questions about the materials being used. If you mat and frame projects at home, always buy archival materials. The backboard, mat, and glazing (usually glass) need to be carefully considered.

Certificates and photos. My parents' wedding certificate was one of those things not framed properly. The mat board used was very acidic, and there was a brownish band along the line where the mat and the certificate met. The space under the mat was also yellow. This is called "mat burn." A dark striped pattern of discoloration was forming evenly through the certificate as well. This was caused by the corrugated cardboard used as a filler or backboard directly behind the certificate. Common cardboard contains lignin and is highly acidic. Everywhere the corrugation touched the certificate, it "burned" a stripe on it. The signatures, signed in blue ink, were fading away.

If you want to avoid such problems, you can follow the steps we used in preserving my parents' wedding certificate:

1. We made several *photocopies* of the certificate.

2. We sprayed the original certificate with a *deacidification spray* (see Chapter 2).

3. We purchased an *acid-free mat board*. A mat board is important because you never want your items touching the glass (or glazing, as it is called). I have seen many photos stuck right to the glass because there was no space between them and the glass.

4. We then removed the cardboard and replaced it with an acid-free piece of *Fome-cor as a filler in the back*.

5. Standard window glass has historically been used in most framing. However, most glass is fragile, heavy, and will not block damaging light rays. There is a conservation glass on the market now that will block harmful ultraviolet rays—make sure that you get the real thing if you choose this alternative. Conservation glass comes in both clear and nonreflective types. For our project we purchased a special *filtering acrylic*. Two appropriate types of acrylic are UF3 Plexiglas, made by Rohm & Haas, and Acrylite OP-2, made by Cyro Industries. These will block out 85 to 95 percent of the ultraviolet rays from sunlight and fluorescent tubes. A disadvantage of acrylics is that they scratch easily, so be careful. Acrylic also has a static charge and attracts particles from artwork such as pastels, graphite, gouache, and tempra. It is best to not use acrylics with these mediums. Another disadvantage is that acrylics tend to have a yellow cast.

6. Where the glass rested in the frame, we glued in *isolation strips* with Elmer's School Glue. The strips are made from a soft, spongy material that helps to keep dirt from entering the front of the frame.

7. We placed the mat board, certificate, and backing in the frame, and after it was all put together we put strips of archival, double-sided tape on the back of the frame to secure a piece of *acid-free paper for a dust cover.* This prevents dust, dirt, insects, and any other foreign matter from entering the frame.

You can follow this same procedure with your valuable certificates, photos, and portraits. Photos and portraits can be treated with a UV spray that will have the same effect as the filtering acrylic. Talk to a custom photography studio about acquiring the spray.

Sometimes an item being framed is smaller than the backboard. Artwork and certificates can be ruined if they are secured to the back mat with masking tape, an oily glue, or spray adhesive. Acid-free tissue hinges should be used. These use a water-activated adhesive that is easily reversible in water. A "T" hinge can also be made from document repair tape, or simply use unbuffered tissue paper coated with wheat starch paste for an adhesive. (Other archival mounting strips and tapes may be used. See appendix for sources.) Archival, double-sided tape should be used when adhering the mat board to the back mat.

Metal frames are archival if they are coated with baked enamel and there is no rust present. Aluminum frames are the best because aluminum is totally inert, lightweight, inexpensive, and unaffected by moisture fluctuations. Stainless steel and brass are safe but heavy and expensive. Any wood frame can be harmful. Raw woods contain oxidizing agents and other chemicals that will stain the mount and may affect the print. Hard woods are better than soft. They have less acid in them. Stained, varnished, or oiled frames should be avoided, as should frames with other finishes that may damage your precious items.

If you really want to use a wood frame, you should paint it with a water-based clear acrylic paint. This will help in coating the tannic acids. However, there are no guaranteed "safe" wood sealers. Aluminum foil can be laid around the inside of a wood frame and fastened around the edges to help prevent acid migration.

Due to the damaging effects of light and temperature, I have framed copies of some valuables and kept the originals in a safer place. Behind the frame, you really have to look closely to see that it is not an original.

Keepsakes. To frame any kind of fabric such as embroidered, crocheted, and tatted items, cover a piece of museum board or Fome-cor with a piece of prewashed cotton muslin. (Washing takes the sizing out.) Don't use glue, but stitch the muslin in place around the board like an envelope. If you like, you can stuff it first with a bit of cotton batting to give it a puffy look. Attach your doily, handkerchief, or whatever you are framing to the covered board by basting all around it with cotton thread. Use a ball-point needle so you won't cut or tear the fabric. Continue framing as explained above, with acid-free mat board and a filtering acrylic or conservation glass. If your article is too thick for a standard frame, a shadow-box frame can be purchased, or you can use frame spacers. Remember to never have your article touching the glass or acrylic.

Blessing dresses look great framed. You'll need a shadow-box frame because of the thickness of the dress. Stuff the dress with acid-free tissue paper to give it some shape. Tack it onto the cotton fabric at the shoulder seams. Be careful to use enough stitches to prevent any stress to the dress. *DO NOT* use a spray adhesive, as some framers do. It will harm the fabric and attach the dress permanently to the backing. Whatever kind of framing you do, you want to make sure that you never harm the article and that the procedure will be reversible.

To frame articles such as eyeglasses, jewelry, or other mementoes, use wire or fishing line to secure the item to the backing. A silicone glue is appropriate for metals such as coins; if you want to take the article out, the glue will peel right off.

Some heirlooms, such as quilts, tapestries, and rugs, look nice displayed on a wall but are too big to be framed. Never hang them with individual rings or safety pins. Items should be hung so that the weight is distributed evenly over many supporting points. Make a casing by hand stitching a piece of prewashed,

100 percent cotton muslin to the top back of the article. Obtain a Plexiglas rod, an aluminum curtain rod, or a wooden dowel coated with a water-based, clear acrylic paint. Thread the rod through the casing, making sure that the rod or dowel is longer than the width of the item being hung. This way the ends can rest into a wall mount or bracket.

You can also use a wide Velcro strip to hang an article. The prickly part of the Velcro should be secured by tacking or stapling it to a sealed wooden board on the wall. Sew the smoother part of the Velcro onto a cotton muslin fabric strip (machine sewing is fine). Then hand sew the strip onto the quilt or rug. When taking the item off the wall, carefully separate the Velcro with your hands. Velcro is strong—if you just try to pull the item off, you could tear your heirloom piece.

Textiles that are too fragile to be hung at one end can be mounted on a covered frame. To make one, stretch a piece of pre-washed cotton muslin around a frame and secure it. Carefully baste stitch the textile onto the fabric stretched on the frame. Sew all around and through the piece, not just at the edges. The fragile piece needs proper support.

Textiles displayed by hanging have no protection from pollutants or light, so make sure that they are hung in an area where the conditions are the best, and rotate them from time to time. (See light and temperature care for heirlooms in this chapter.) Never mount a fragile item without some kind of protection from dust, pollutants, and light. Sometimes museums mount an acrylic box over the top of an item to protect it.

A Keepsake Box

There are some heirlooms that I don't keep on display. I keep some special things together in an archival storage box. Each member of the family has his or her own box, containing such items as medals, a Primary bandlo, hospital bracelets, booties, mission mementoes, and so on. Be sure, if you do this, that you have an inventory list, as discussed earlier. Also, be sure to store your box in the right environment, as has also been discussed.

Creating Your Own Heirlooms

Create some heirlooms for your own posterity. Whether you like to sew, make pottery, build with wood, or quilt, these pieces will be valuable to your children and grandchildren someday. Keep a record of things that are sentimental to you so that you can pass them on to others.

I knew a woman who was dying of cancer. Knowing that she would never see any of her grandchildren in this life, she made baby blankets for each of her children to use for the children they would have someday.

When sewing clothes or quilts, there are several things you can do to help future generations keep your articles healthy. Keep a pocket on the back of a quilt with samples of the different fabrics and threads used. This way, colorfast tests can be done without disturbing the quilt itself, and tears in the quilt can be mended with those fabric pieces. You can accomplish the same thing by setting aside a box of fabric pieces from sewing projects. Also record the type of material that was used.

Heirlooms can be made from existing items. For example, I saw a beautifully framed sampler made from pieces of a grandfather's ties. Many people make patchwork quilts from old clothes. A quilt that is definitely not salvageable can still be remembered: Frame a piece of it, or make a pillow. You can dry flowers from sentimental occasions and turn them into sachets, put them in perfume bottles, arrange them under a dome, or frame them. I saw a beautiful frame that had a portrait of a bride along with dried flowers from the wedding. The list is endless. A little imagination can turn any item into something unique.

Use caution when altering an item. For example, if Grandpa had only three ties, don't cut them up. But if his favorites are saved and you still have a lot left, go ahead and make a sampler. Never make a patchwork quilt out of heirloom pieces that have great sentimental or monetary value left as is. The original condition of an article is most often the best way to preserve it.

AUDIO AND VIDEO RECORDINGS

*If a picture is worth a thousand words,
a moving picture with sound ought to be
worth at least twice that!*

We live in a time when technological advances offer easy and incredible new ways to preserve histories. Wouldn't it be amazing if the Mormon pioneers or Nephi in the Book of Mormon had been able to use a video camera or a tape recorder?

Video cameras are wonderful at capturing an individual's emotions, voice, gestures, and facial expressions. Audio tape recorders are very convenient and offer a handy, quick way to record feelings.

What Should I Record?

Obviously, special events are natural times for filming or recording: weddings, funerals, missionary farewells, talks, birthday parties, graduations, vacations, dance recitals, ball games, school programs, and even births. I was so thrilled when I heard my baby's heartbeat inside me for the first time that at my next appointment I tape recorded it. (This is one of those things that just can't be transcribed onto paper.)

Although I love special occasions, my favorite videos are often of spontaneous occurrences. Try taping the daily routine of getting the kids off to school, washing the car, playing with the kids, and visiting the neighbors. Everyday life will be of great interest to your posterity. Record about your own life those memories you wish you had of your grandparents' and parents' lives. These will in turn become treasures to your posterity.

It is also fun to go on a traveling video adventure. Film the homes you've lived in, schools and churches you've attended, yards and fields you played in as a child, places of employment, local landmarks, or any other places where you've spent time.

Benefits

1. Audio and video histories capture a personality and sense of humor better than the written word. It has been said that a picture is worth a thousand words. A talking picture is worth even more!

2. Video and audio recordings are quick and easy. Many people have tried and tried to get their personal histories down on paper and just never seem to succeed. I heard of one stake that took a giant step in helping its members record their personal histories. They supplied members of the stake with a general outline listing common events in a typical life. They then set aside a day, provided a video camera, and had members of the stake come and record their lives. In that one day, many families made great strides in creating personal histories. Not only that, but many also experienced a positive introduction to one type of history recording and have since moved into other areas with excitement.

3. Many people like to take videos of pictures and mementoes that relate to events and experiences so they can tell about those experiences in a more meaningful way. One example of this is to videotape a stack of children's artwork, school papers, or projects with the children narrating. (Then you can throw those papers and Popsicle-stick towers away!) What a wonderful way to do your personal history!

4. With a videotape, many documents, mementoes, keepsakes, and heirlooms can be shown and discussed. This way they can also be shared with other family members. Many of these

items are unique and cannot be divided or shared in any other way than by sharing them on video. For example, my family owns a wonderful old parlor chair that was my dad's when he was a child. Only one of the seven children will end up with the chair, but we can all have photos and videos of this and other keepsakes.

5. Video and audio narration can easily be transcribed and preserved in written form.

6. A video or audio tape can be inexpensively copied to share with others.

7. Photos, slides, and old movies can be transferred onto videotape for easy viewing. It costs less to videotape a quantity of old photos or slides than to have duplicate prints made. Narration and even music can then be added to the video to describe the photos being shown and enhance the setting.

8. Although the resolution of super 8 movie film is of higher quality than that of the standard VHS videotape, the film often has problems over the years. (However, high 8 video and the new digital video are better than movie film.) As film ages it gets brittle, cracks, and often breaks. Sometimes the sprocket holes that feed it through the projector break as well. The price of movie film and processing is about $20 for three minutes' worth. If the high resolution of movie film is desired, however, copy the movie onto a videocassette for frequent viewing and keep the original for use on special occasions. Frequent projection of movie film hastens the deterioration because of the exposure to the projector light.

Cautions and Hints

Both video and audio tapes are magnetic, and unfortunately, no magnetic recording medium is permanent. Estimates of the longevity from manufacturers have been evasive. Tape manufacturers don't discuss it much. The technology is new, and there is no way of knowing how long a modern videocassette consisting of cobalt ferric oxide or metallic particles inside a plastic shell will hold its image intact. Professionals have had only twenty years of experience with traditional oxide tapes; the newer metal tape, introduced with the Video 8 formats in 1985, is still in its infancy.

So, what's the bottom line? How long will a video or audio cassette last? Experts say that with proper care and storage, they can last up to fifteen years without any significant degradation. Now, this doesn't mean they will suddenly be destroyed in fifteen years. It means that they may start showing signs of degradation, and the subject of time is still a matter of debate. We do know, however, that the better they are taken care of, the longer they will last. To ensure the best recordings and storage environment, keep in mind the following cautions and procedures.

1. Extremes in humidity cause adverse effects on tapes. Low humidity brings about increased amounts of airborne dust, debris, and static, which can contaminate and scratch tapes. High humidity causes increased absorption of moisture. Dramatic changes or cycling in humidity alter the tape dimensions and may cause increased friction in the recorder tape path. For optimal operation and storage of audio and video tapes, the relative humidity level should be between 40 and 60 percent.

2. Closely associated with humidity is temperature. The ideal temperature for tape is from 65 to 70 degrees F. Fluctuations in temperature are hard on tape because of expansion and contraction of the base film. A hot, wet environment is very deteriorating. If a tape has been subjected to this, it should be placed in a cool, dry (low-moisture) environment for several days before use. No matter what the environment the tape was recorded in, the tape should always be rewound in the environment in which it is to be stored. If a tape has been stored at a low temperature, it should sit for a few hours at 65 to 70 degrees F. before it is used.

3. Contamination is tape's worst enemy, but tension is a close second. Before a tape is used, relieve variations in tape stress by fast-forwarding through the entire tape and then rewinding it. It is important to do this with unused tape straight from the manufacturer. When you are finished recording, fast-forward to the end, then rewind without stopping. Stopping in the middle will

cause uneven pack stresses. Fast-forward and rewind all your tapes at least once every three years. This will release strains and adhesions caused by storage.

4. Airport security walk-through and X-ray scan systems *will not* demagnetize tape. However, hand-held metal detectors can demagnetize tape. Be careful! Don't be confused: This is totally opposite of what is good for photographic film. (It's the X-ray equipment that hurts photo film.) Use a nonmagnetic storage container or wrap tapes in aluminum foil to help prevent any demagnetization.

5. Allow the VCR, tape player, and video and audio cassettes to warm up for two hours before using them when bringing them in from a cold environment. Wrapping them in plastic bags when taking them out in the cold gives added protection. Water condensation will form on the outside of the bag rather than on the equipment or cassettes.

6. Avoid dropping tapes. The sudden shock can cause the tape pack to shift, causing binding or jamming in the shell.

7. Avoid touching the actual tape. Oils from your skin can ruin a good recording. The oils can also attract other dirt, which can eventually damage the tape heads.

Recording

1. **Be familiar with your machines and recorders.** Read your manuals. Practice determining the best recording volume, distance, and light for your machine. Tapes are often "eaten" by the machines because proper care was not taken, or the machine was not used correctly.

2. Whenever you can, **plug in your recorder** rather than recording under battery power. Batteries can fade or die at any time. Many important occasions have been lost because of dead batteries. Weak batteries sometimes fail to record a strong sync track.

3. **Use external microphones if possible.** External microphones are preferable to internal ones for two reasons. First, an internal microphone picks up the sounds of the machine's motor,

so the recording has a dull hum in the background. Second, external microphones are generally of a better quality.

4. **Be aware of noises** around you that interfere with the sounds you are recording. Traffic, television, doorbells, and phones are all distractions. Things we don't usually think about can also cause muffling, such as the motor on the refrigerator. Simple talking can ruin a good video. For example, when my friend's brother was taping some shots of her wedding, two sisters were talking in the background about good places to eat lunch. Of course, the sisters were unaware of the microphone. Their conversation was very distracting.

5. **Use erasure prevention tabs and switches!** A woman once told me she had videotaped her parents' fiftieth wedding anniversary celebration, and then later that weekend her children accidentally used the tape to record a TV show. Obviously, she was very upset. To prevent this from happening to you, pop out the erasure insets so that the tape cannot be erased or re-recorded. These safety tabs are located on the edge or spine of the tapes. (There are two of them on an audiocassette, one for side A and the other for side B. When you are looking at side A, the tab for it is on the left. There is only one tab on a VHS or Beta videotape, because there is only one recording side.) If for any reason you want to add more recordings to the tape, place a piece of adhesive tape over the slot. The recorder just needs to "sense" something there—the "something" doesn't need to be plastic. On an 8mm cassette there is a switch that can be moved between positions so that you can record later.

6. When recording, **never start right at the beginning of a tape.** On an audiocassette there are a few inches of leader tape that cannot be recorded on. Many people have lost the first bit of a recording by trying to record when the leader tape was playing. It is important, however, to wind in a bit past the leader tape for a few seconds before recording as well. This helps prevent contamination and physical damage that sometimes come near the beginning of the tape. This will also help to avoid "drop-out," the fading in or out of the sound or picture. Remember, anytime

the tape is exposed, there is a chance for contamination. This is another reason to rewind completely before you take the tape out.

Videotapes have little or no leader tape at the beginning. Because of this, it is very important to run the tape for a few seconds—even up to a half a minute—at the beginning before recording. Not only does this bypass any contamination, but it ensures that the heads are engaged and the sync track is strong.

7. For important, irreplaceable tapes, **make duplicate copies** (preferably to a digital format) from the master tape every three to five years. These copies, though down a generation, will at least provide insurance against any deterioration or failure of the original master. Each time a copy is made, it moves down a generation. The original is the first generation; the copy is the second generation; a copy of the copy is the third generation. Always make copies from a first-generation tape if possible. If "A" is the original and "B" is the first copy, it makes sense that a copy "C" made from "B" will not be as high in quality as if it were made from "A." However, when you copy digitally, no distortion occurs from copy to copy.

Playing

1. **Avoid using tapes where they might contact any foreign or sticky substance.** These things will contaminate not only the tape but also the head and tape path in your machine. This in turn can contaminate other tapes played in that machine. Old tapes may have decay from the glue that holds the oxide recording medium. This glue can stick to the heads of the machine and damage the next tape.

2. If problems occur while playing a cassette, you should **examine it for damage.** On an audiotape, carefully look at the exposed tape. On a videotape, open the cassette guard panel (being careful not to touch the exposed tape). Don't use the tape if it is damaged. Some signs to look for are wrinkles on the edge or middle, creases, scratches, tears, or broken tape.

Cleaning

It is important to clean the heads on your VCR and tape players. A good contact between the tape and the video or play heads is critical in obtaining good picture and sound quality. If tapes run for a long time without any cleaning, minute particles and dust from either the tape itself or the environment can accumulate and become attached to the heads. This greatly degrades the quality of picture and sound. These harmful materials also can scratch the tapes played on the machines. Some recorder heads have a gap of less than 1.5 microns between poles. Dirt or other pollutants lodged in this gap as well as on the pinch rollers, capstans, and glide paths can cause irreparable damage. Cleaning removes these materials, which in return helps to prevent tapes from scratching. Cleaning should be done every thirty to fifty hours of playing or recording—more often if you have to factor in dust and smoke, a poor quality tape, or frequent and prolonged stop-frame usage. I've been told it is also a good idea to clean after using any rental tape. These bring in outside contaminants from other machines. Follow the instructions on the cleaner you buy. Don't hesitate to buy a more expensive cleaner that is recommended by a professional. Some commercial head cleaners are abrasive to the heads, especially for high-quality VCRs. A professional may be able to show you how to manually clean your own machine. Make sure you allow at least five minutes of drying time after you use a tape head cleaner before you load a tape.

Storing Tapes

1. When storing a tape for a long period of time, **fast-forward to the end and then rewind without stopping.** This will help to ensure an even tension throughout the tape. Never remove tapes from the machine in the middle of the reel—the exposed section can become damaged or contaminated. (This is why audiotapes have a leader tape at the beginning. Always store them with that leader tape showing.) Dust, fingerprints, oils from

hands, and scratches on the tape cause "drop-out." (This refers to the sound or picture fading in and out.) Wherever the tape is smudged, the play head can't read it. An oily residue also attracts other contaminants, which will migrate along the tape each time it is played. These contaminants can also be left on the play head itself, in turn contaminating other tapes.

2. **Never leave tapes in your camera or machines.** Leaving them threaded (even overnight) can sometimes reshape the tape to the threading path. This can cause picture and sound distortion.

3. **Store tapes in their cases vertically, on their edge, never lying flat.** This helps prevent damage to the edge of the tape. When tapes lie flat for a long period of time, they tend to slide down and rest on the bottom reel or flange. This is what manufacturers call "hub-drop." When tapes are stored vertically on their edge, the tape rests on itself. You can visualize this by thinking of the big reels of film in an old movie theater. If they were stored on their side, due to gravity, the tape would slide to the bottom reel. If stored upright, the tape rolls evenly on itself and the hub. Audio and video tapes are simply little reels in a box. It's also a good idea to periodically change end for end when storing tapes for a long time. And from a practical standpoint, it is easier to retrieve a tape that is stored vertically than to try to pull one out from the bottom of a stack!

4. A magnetic head was used to record or arrange the pattern on the tape ribbon in the first place, so, obviously, external magnetic fields can affect the signal on the tape. Because of this, **store tapes away from magnetic fields** such as amplifiers, motors, magnets, voltage transformers, telephones, typewriters, appliances, and speakers. (In fact, a speaker is simply a big magnet.) Magnetism can erase or rearrange the tape's encoded magnetic pattern. Many people keep their videos and cassettes by their TV and stereo systems. They should be stored at least ten feet away from any of these appliances. I once ruined a tape simply by having it come in contact with a refrigerator-door magnet.

Nonmagnetic storage containers are available for long-term

187

storage or shipping. Wrapping aluminum foil around the tape is also a magnetic deterrent. The aluminum prevents the magnetic field from changing.

5. **Store tapes in plastic, dust-free cases** rather than cardboard ones. Plastic cases are stronger and will lessen impact if dropped and minimize physical damage to tape edges. Most plastic cases have space where the tape can breathe, which is good. A tightly fit, totally sealed storage container would eliminate dust and other particles, but would not allow the air exchange that tapes need.

6. **Store tapes out of the sun.** A sunny dashboard is almost certain death to a tape. I keep my most valuable recordings in a fireproof box.

7. **Label your tapes well** with names, dates, and places. Continue to update the label whenever you add to or delete from the recordings. It is very helpful to include the length of each recorded segment as well as its beginning location on the tape. For example:

Ceciley's First Birthday, May 14, 1991, 00:05:20 to 00:52:08

Grandma Young's Story Time, August 2, 1994, 00:52:08 to 01:23:19

Specifics about Audiocassettes

One of my favorite jobs was transcribing a journal for a man. His commute was about forty-five minutes a day, and as he rode he would dictate his journal into a tape recorder. Later I would transcribe it for him. This way he had not only a written journal but his voice as well.

When my dad died, I had many thoughts and feelings swelling up inside. I knew that I needed to record these things while they were fresh on my mind, but the last thing I felt like doing was writing. So, late one night I sat up and talked and cried into a tape recorder. Later I transcribed the tape, but I am thankful to have the audio recording, because a lot of the emotion and feeling didn't come through in the written form.

While my husband was on his mission, the family turned on

the tape recorder and left it running during Thanksgiving dinner one year. This tape is especially valuable now because it contains the voices of two sisters-in-law, a niece, and my husband's father, all of whom have since died.

Some recordings, such as my babies' heartbeats when I was pregnant, are impossible to transcribe. This makes them even more valuable. Make multiple copies of these irreplaceable tapes and store them in separate places in case one is destroyed.

For Christmas one year, my mother bought books for my children and then read the stories onto audiocassettes for them. It's fun for my children to sit down and listen to Grandma read to them whenever they want. When a friend found that her mother had only three months to live, she had her mother read her favorite children's stories onto a cassette. She wanted her unborn children to hear their grandmother reading stories to them.

Tapes are a great aid in the interviewing process for personal and family histories, as was discussed in Chapter 5. Audio-cassettes are handy and easy to use. Try to think of times when you can use yours!

Hints and Tips for Audiocassettes

1. A tape recorder placed on a hard surface often rattles or sounds hollow. Resting the tape recorder on a soft surface often produces a better sounding tape. Experiment.

2. Buy the best tape you can. *Bias* is a term used to describe a tape's quality and lack of signal distortion. The higher the bias, the better the quality.

Basically, audiocassettes come in four varieties. The first kind of tape, the least expensive, is a Normal bias tape. These tapes are basic and can handle any simple voice recording. The second kind of tape is a Ferric-Chromide (FeCr). This is a Medium bias tape. Two coating layers with different forces are used to make these: One is superior for high frequencies, and the other handles mid and low ranges well. These are great for music because they capture a whole range of frequencies. The third tape is a High bias or Chrome (CrO_2). These are great at capturing the subtle frequencies in music. They also have ultra-fine magnetic particles that suppress the irritating hiss noise of cassettes. The fourth kind is a Metal bias. Modulation and print-through noise are very low, meaning that any background "hiss" is very minimal. The metal particles give these tapes double the sound quality of a Chrome tape. The signal-to-noise ratio is higher on a Metal tape as well. It's safe to say that a Metal bias tape is of far better quality than a Normal bias one. For this reason, I would choose to use this kind of a tape for my important recording.

3. If your recorder offers options in bias/equalization settings, use the proper setting for recording each type of cassette. For example, a Metal bias tape is type IV; a Normal bias would be type I.

4. The smaller the amount of time on a tape, the better the tape is. For example, the following table shows on the average the thickness and signal-to-noise ratio of each size of tape.

Minutes	30–60	90	120
Thickness	.67 mil	.46 mil	.35 mil
Breaking Strength	3.2 lbs.	2.1 lbs.	1.2 lbs.
Signal-to-Noise Ratio	59.0 dB	57.0 dB	54.0 dB

As you can see, a 120-minute tape is a lot thinner than a 60-minute one. The thinner the tape, the more chance of breaking and jamming. A thinner tape is also more susceptible to what is called "bleed-through" or "print-through." This is when the magnetic particles change patterns and you hear side A of the tape when you are listening to side B.

When recording, you want the highest signal-to-noise ratio possible. The signal is what you are recording. The noise is the hiss or hum on the blank tape. The smaller the amount of time on the tape, the less noise.

5. Another good rule is to buy tapes with a cassette shell that is screwed together, not glued. It is much easier to take apart

screws than glue when fixing or splicing a tape. When splicing, always use audiotape splicing material.

6. Keep cassettes in their hub-lock boxes when not in use to avoid loose tape winds. This is especially important in the car.

7. Gently take up the slack on the tape by turning the hub by hand before inserting the cassette in the recorder.

8. If you have had several problems with tapes jamming, stretching, or showing damage, have your recorder alignment checked by a reliable technician.

9. If noise reduction (DBX/Dolby) is used in recording, it should also be used in playback. However, Dolby C will enhance any recording whether used in the playback or not.

Specifics about Video Recordings

I like to use a video camera with editing capabilities. We have an 8mm camera, which plays smaller tapes that have a better resolution than a regular VHS tape. They can be played through the camera, an 8mm VCR, or transcribed and edited onto a VHS tape. (This last option loses some of the resolution of the original.)

I had an interesting experience that gave me an insight into the benefits of editing. We took our video camera to the birth of my first child, Ceciley. I specifically told the nurse who was videotaping that I didn't want any "X-rated" shots. I wanted only the baby after she was born. Well, when we viewed the tape later that evening, I was shocked and very upset. She got the whole birth on tape! I was frustrated. I didn't want anyone to see that.

My dear husband said: "Anita, this is great! We can edit and transfer over to a VHS tape the 'G-rated' things and keep the 8mm tape 'for our eyes only.'" Well, it has been so great having that 8mm tape. Being on the other end of things, I didn't get to see the birth, so it was very interesting to view it on the tape.

When it was close to time for me to deliver my second child, I was very grateful to be able to view the video of the first birth to prepare myself. So when that second child, Joseph, was born, I had the nurse videotape the whole birth for me. These tapes are

AUDIO AND VIDEO RECORDINGS

so special and valuable to me. The 8mm is truly for me and my husband only, and the edited part is fun to share with others. Just a hint, though: Try to have the person who is filming get fairly long segments of "G-rated" material so you don't have to edit out valuable conversations.

Hints and Tips for Videos

1. Use a tripod when filming to keep the camera steady.

2. Buy the best tape you can. A super high grade tape will give better quality than a standard VHS tape. Read the section on audiocassette quality; the same reasoning applies here.

3. Record on SP (short play), not EP (extended play), for important, valuable recordings. For example, a typical 120 VHS will give you 2 hours on SP versus 6 hours on EP. When the tape runs fast, more film per second is capturing your image, making a better quality picture. When I'm recording things that I really don't care about, such as the news or a TV show to watch later, I record on extended play to squeeze as much onto the tape as possible. But I want recordings for historical purposes to be as clear as possible, so I always use short play for those.

4. Have someone mention the date, place, and occasion you are filming.

5. Remember that video is a moving picture! Film action shots. Formal poses are nice from time to time, but take advantage of the action possibilities.

6. Videotapes can be a chronological collection of your family's life, or they can be made according to topics and subjects. For example, each child could have his or her own video with things on it that are special to that child. You could make a Christmas video, or one of just birthdays. These show the holiday or birthday chronologically over time. A vacation or other special event could be the subject of its own tape. Videos can also be a compilation of photos from the past.

7. Videotapes are a great way to record and capture precious keepsakes and heirlooms for history's sake. It is also a good idea to make such a recording for insurance purposes. After you have

made a tape, keep it in a safety deposit box or give a copy to a family member living in another home in case of a disaster.

Care of Phonograph Records

Some of us still have old LP records. If any of these hold value for you, they should be transferred to a cassette or CD. But they are still enjoyable to have around. All phonograph records—whether they are vinyl, shellac, glass, aluminum, or cardboard based—are subject to warping, breakage, scratching, or other surface damage. In caring for them, make sure that they are stored out of strong light and heat. Dust and dirt particles cause scratches, so keep albums away from ventilation ducts and other areas with debris. For long-term storage, keep them in a cool, dark place and store them vertically with sturdy supports, never stacked horizontally. Store records by size to reduce the possibility of warping. Avoid packing them too tightly.

Archival boxes and sleeves made especially for record storage can be purchased. They are excellent for segregating fragile and damaged records as well.

Care of Movie Film

Many of us have old home movies that hold sentimental value. The best thing to do with them is to have them transferred to a VHS video and then re-created digitally when you can. The original movie, however, should still be kept. (Copies from originals are usually better than those made from a second-generation copy.) The resolution of movie film is of a higher quality than that of standard VHS tape. As film ages, however, it gets brittle, cracks, and often breaks. Proper storage can slow down this process and help the film last as long as possible.

Permanent storage of movie film requires low temperatures, from 0 to 40 degrees F., with controlled relative humidity of 25 to 40 percent. One of the biggest problems for movie film is that when it gets too hot, the tape shrinks and consequently so do the sprocket holes. If the sprockets won't fit and feed through the movie projector, it is impossible to view the movie.

Light is very damaging to film as well. Not only does it promote fading of the image, but it dries the film and causes it to become brittle. Hence, frequent projection of a movie hastens the deterioration, because heat and light are both involved in showing the movie. It's a good idea to transfer a copy onto a video for viewing and save the original in a safe place.

Movies should be stored in vented polypropylene film cans or vapor-permeable cardboard containers. This helps to prevent the "vinegar syndrome" of films rotting. Sealed or metal containers accelerate both dye fading and film-base deterioration of acetate-base films. Metal containers have known to rust and corrode, causing damage to their contents. For long-term storage, films should be removed from their flanges and wound on archival film cores to prevent warping and edge damage. The best film containers are vented, so take precautions to keep the storage area filtered and free of dust, lint, and other pollutants.

No matter how faded a film may be, never discard it. Copies from originals are usually the best choice. A professional can help with computer-aided colorization to reconstruct the faded dye images.

Cellulose nitrate film is very dangerous. This old film, which was produced until 1951, can spontaneously combust and burn very rapidly, destroying your home. You can read more about cellulose nitrate film in Chapter 7, "Photographs, Slides, and Negatives."

Reel-to-Reel Audiotapes

Storage of reel-to-reel tapes is a cross between audiocassette storage and movie film care. First, reel-to-reel tapes are magnetic and susceptible to the same environmental damage as a smaller cassette tape. Follow the precautions recommended for audiocassettes. Store tapes vertically and be sure that the tape pack is even and smooth.

Second, the storage boxes used for reel-to-reel tapes should be like the ones used for movie film. Boxes should close tightly to keep dust out but be "breathable" to allow enough air to exchange and retard "vinegar syndrome." Sealed metal cans can rust and do not allow air circulation. A sturdy, reinforced, acid-free, buffered storage box is the best.

Digital Recording

Digital recordings come in several formats. A laser disc is digital. So is a compact disc, or CD. There are digital audiotapes (DAT), and now a digital videotape has come onto the market. A digital recording offers better quality than an analog one. If it is at all possible, valuable tapes should be transferred to a digital format. However, even though digital is a superior recording medium, digital audio and video tapes are still subject to the normal deterioration problems associated with tapes.

It used to be that the process of digital recording onto a compact disc (CD) was rather expensive and not typically something that was done at home. Today digital recorders and cameras are more widely available and somewhat more affordable. (See more about digital cameras in Chapter 11, "Computers.")

If at all possible, transfer your sentimental and valuable videos and audiocassettes onto a CD. For storage and care of compact discs, see Chapter 11, "Computers."

Staying Current

With the rapid development of video and audio recording technology, the possibility of the current machines being readily available in fifty to a hundred years is highly unlikely. This isn't hard to understand. I have some old reel-to-reel tape recordings of my family and no reel-to-reel tape player to play them on. I also have old 8-track tapes and no 8-track tape player. Many people have old super 8 movie film and no projector. My nephew has some great films on Beta and no machine to view them. As new technology arises, make sure to transfer your valuable audio and video recordings to the updated system. For example, I have some LP recordings of choirs I sang in during high school. Years ago I transferred them to a cassette tape because they were sounding scratchy. I am now in the process of having them recorded digitally onto a CD. In years to come, if CDs start to become outdated, I will transfer them to whatever medium is current then. If we take care of our tapes as well as we can and keep up with technology, we will be able to view and hear our histories forever.

COMPUTERS

"We have been greatly blessed with the material means, the technology, and an inspired message. . . . More is expected of us than any previous generation."

EZRA TAFT BENSON

In 1989 I picked up a science book in an elementary school library. The particular chapter I was reading described astronomy and future possible space travel. I was shocked when I read, "Someday man may even walk on the moon!" Obviously, the book was way out of date.

When I think about computers, I am often reminded of this story. Any specifics regarding computers that I write today will probably be outdated by the time you read this. After all, it wasn't so long ago that we were using slide rules instead of calculators. So I am going to be as general as I can in my writing here. Although technology will change, the basics may remain somewhat the same. Countless books and magazines are available to keep you updated.

No sooner do you master your latest electronic "toy" or "plug-em-in" than something better has replaced it. As electrical devices go, nothing has changed our lives more than the computer. I remember baby-sitting about twenty-five years ago at a home that had a basement room we were to keep out of. In that room was a computer! This machine took up the whole room. I was in awe of this family that seemed so space-aged because they had a computer. Today it is not uncommon for a family to have several computers. Some are small and can be carried around wherever you go.

Computers in one form or another are here to stay. They are valuable tools in the home, workplace, and for preservation purposes as well. This chapter will discuss how they can help you preserve your memories.

Journals and Histories

A computer is the best typewriter/word processor you could ever have. Computers can help you write your journals and histories with ease. When I began writing this book, I had what I felt was a very good typewriter/word processor. It had a correcting ribbon and could save up to ten documents. I loved this typewriter. I felt comfortable with the keyboard, had learned the commands, and was unwilling to change. So I started out typing my book.

My husband, an engineer, has a very nice computer at work. He has been aware of the wonder and value of computers ever since they became common in the workplace. He tried for years to bring me into the modern world and get a computer at home. I could never quite catch the picture. He had a nice computer at work; I had my nice typewriter; why would we need a computer at home?

Well, as I was writing, I wanted to edit. I cannot even tell you how difficult it was to insert a paragraph, change a sentence, or even correct the spelling of one word! Joe kept saying, "Anita, you need a computer!" I kept saying, "I don't have time to *learn* the computer." I had taken a difficult computer class years ago in college, and I didn't want to lose several months while trying to learn another complicated machine. (After all, my typewriter had taken a while to figure out.)

Joe eventually won, and we bought a computer. I confess now that I don't have time to *not* have a computer. Today, basic computers are such a cinch to learn to use. I have great admiration for anyone who wrote a book before computers were available for general use. How did they do it? I doubt I would have had the patience to write and edit on my old typewriter what I have done on my computer.

Why have I shared this story with you? Because through this process I have learned what you probably already know: the value of simple word processing with computers. My journal and personal history are so much easier to write now that I have a computer. Corrections and changes are a piece of cake! It's easy and fun to use different fonts and formats, graphics and photos. I love the thesaurus and the spelling checker. The options available on the computer are mind-boggling.

Hints and Cautions

1. For journals and histories, make sure that you use an acid-free, buffered paper in your printer.

2. You may want to look into the software packages specifically designed for writing journals and personal and family histories.

3. Not all printers have archival inks. Remember that an ink needs to be permanent, fade proof, chemical proof, and waterproof to be archival. *Generally speaking,* a dot matrix printer is not permanent. An ink or bubble jet printer "sprays" the ink onto the paper; it is light and fade resistant but not waterproof. Laser printers offer the archival qualities. The ink from a laser printer is heat set, fused into the paper, not just on top of it.

4. Use a backup to save your work. *Always print and make a hard copy.* The best backup you can do is to make a printed copy. You don't have to ask around very far to find someone who has lost data or even had a hard drive crash. (Before this book went to press, I lost *my* hard drive, and with it some of my corrections. Thank goodness the body of the book was already finished!) If you don't have copies or a backup, all can be lost.

Books of Remembrance and Genealogy

Genealogy is the second most popular hobby in America, next to gardening. Millions of people are interested in their genealogy. Because of this, there are countless software packages available to help users put together pedigree charts and family trees. These programs are very easy for anyone to use.

Scanners are also nice for copying original documents, thus preserving a person's handwriting.

If you have access to the Internet on your computer, you have access to another valuable resource. There are places that send free monthly E-mail genealogy newsletters. Many people have found connections through the E-mail and located "lost" ancestors. Also, family history centers around the world are linked to the LDS Church's Family History Library.

Photographs

Photography is one area that has been affected drastically by computers. Thanks to scanners and simple software programs, copying and restoring old photographs is easy. A torn, scratched photo can be scanned into the computer and digitally made to look as good as new. Scanners are especially helpful in making copies of photographs for which there are no negatives. There are also scanners made especially for slides.

Many film developers can reproduce your photos onto a floppy disk or CD. You can still receive your regular prints and negatives, but in addition receive all the photo images on a disk. Each floppy disk may hold up to forty photos. CDs may hold hundreds. The software program provided with your photo disk is very simple to use and is like watching a slide show on your computer. Your photos can be imported onto other documents, sent through a modem, or made into a screen saver. The images are stored digitally and will never fade or be subjected to the other environmental problems that regular prints encounter. When you print your photos, it's good to remember that your copies will be only as good as your printer. Use acid-free, buffered paper when printing and your copies will probably out-last your regular photographic prints.

One of the nicest things about a scanner is that it allows many people to have copies of photos that they otherwise would not possess. For example, a friend of mine wanted copies of some ancestors' photos. His aunt was very possessive and wouldn't let the photos out of her sight to have a negative made. But my friend invited her (and her photos) over for lunch, scanned the photos into his computer while she watched, and everyone was happy!

Digital cameras are remarkable. The difference between these and regular cameras is that with a digital camera, film and developing are never involved. The camera reproduces the image digitally onto a computer disk or an on-board memory chip. You then pop the disk or hook the camera into your computer to transfer the images to it. When you print the images, the quality of the output depends on the quality of your printer, but the digitally saved image will not deteriorate with time and can be reproduced often without being changed. The cameras used to be a bit pricey, but you can get one now pretty reasonably, and it won't be long before they are even more affordable.

A person who takes a lot of pictures would likely be able to justify the expense of a digital camera based on the fact that film and developing costs almost disappear. At regular film and developing prices of about $10 to $20 per roll, it doesn't take long to make up the additional cost of the camera.

One drawback to putting digital images on your computer is that they take up a lot of space on a hard drive. Another is that with the rapid changes in technology, your hardware may become obsolete, making your software unusable. Again, as with other items stored on computer media, make backups and printed copies in case of hardware failure.

Audio and Video

This is another area where computers have made a big difference. One of my favorite gadgets is a little machine that hooks up to your computer and then to a VCR, camcorder, or TV. As you watch the movie or video on the computer screen, you can hit a button at any time and presto, the moving image is turned into a high-resolution still print. Many photographers are using this method for the "perfect" shot. You can videotape a group for a few minutes, for example, and then choose the frame in which *everyone* had his or her eyes open.

I am thrilled with this hardware. My camera wasn't working very well the day my son was born. The video of the birth, however, is super. I can now get great photos from the video for his scrapbook.

A year ago, buying a CD recorder for your home computer use would have cost you $1000 or more. Today you can buy some CD recorders for under $500. (Again, by the time you read this, the price could be less than that. This is a good example of how rapidly technology is changing.)

CD recorders are remarkable. Portions from laser discs, video or audio tapes, images, and photographs can easily be transferred onto a CD. The digital recording on CD will outlast the shelf life of the video or audio tape by at least two or three times. (There is no official data as to exactly how long a CD will last.) You can create original work on the discs as well as use them for back-ups. Again, one drawback to this is that a big hard drive is needed to store moving images to the computer itself.

Some software can store LP records and other audiotapes onto a computer's hard drive. All you need is a sound card. One friend had an uncle who was a country and western singer. Before he died, he threw away reels of tape because he was embarrassed by it. Later, my friend gathered old 45 records of his uncle's songs from fourteen different people. He has since converted this music to his computer's hard drive and then onto CDs. A separate software package allowed him to change the mono tracks to stereo tracks. Everyone in the family was delighted.

Scrapbooks

There are many software packages that have clip art and borders great for decorating scrapbook pages. Personally, I have fun just using the different fonts to write text for my books. Scrapbook pages can also be scanned into a computer and printed out or saved on disk for archiving. This is handy if you have more than one book that a page would fit in. For example, you might make a nice page of your two children at the zoo. Instead of making a duplicate page of your borders, stickers, and prints, you could make a copy of the page. Here again, your page would be only as good as your printer.

Software is now available for those who want to put their scrapbooks and family photo albums on CD. An added benefit is that you can also include video and sound clips. Storage on CD allows you to protect your precious photos from many environmental factors, organize them with a searchable index, and keep them in a small space. An electronic scrapbook can be transmitted via modem to family and friends much less expensively than making and sending copies of your photos. In order to take full advantage of these software applications, the user must own a scanner and CD recorder or purchase the service.

Heirlooms and Keepsakes

Photos and descriptions of your priceless heirlooms can be scanned in and described on a computer disk. You can then store a copy of this disk somewhere outside your home for safekeeping. This is an excellent thing to do for insurance purposes.

You can easily create a spreadsheet on the computer to use as your heirloom inventory list. Updating or revising the list is a snap on the computer. Just make sure that you print out a copy to keep in a safe place.

Storage and Care of Discs

Compact discs. Although CDs are generally pretty sturdy, damage can occur. This happens most often when you are transferring the CD from the case to the computer and back. Proper care can protect against warping, scratches, and other damage. CD-Rs, or writable CDs, are even more susceptible to damage. Take extra care when handling them. Interestingly, the shelf life of an unrecorded CD is only about five to ten years. When data is stored on the CD, its shelf life is extended to seventy to a hundred years.

A CD records on the side opposite the label side—this is the most important side to protect. Never touch the surface of the disc or place the recorded side facedown on a hard surface. If you do have to set it down, be sure the recorded side is faceup, and don't put anything on top of it. This will help protect the recording surface from scratches, fingerprints, dust particles, and smears. Hold the disc along the outer edges or by placing your index finger in the center hole. When removing a CD from a plastic case, place the case on a flat surface and gently lift the disc with one hand while pushing on the hub with the thumb or index finger of your other hand. Be careful not to bend the CD.

Debris from your disc drive can scratch the coating on a CD. Make sure that you clean your drive every twenty to forty hours of working.

To clean the discs, use a soft, dry cloth and ethyl alcohol or commercial cleaners made for discs. Always wipe the disc from the center hub in a straight line toward the outside edge. Never wipe in a circular motion. Do not use LP record cleaners, anti-static agents, benzine, or lacquer thinner. These may damage the recording surface.

The temperature and humidity levels safe for CDs are more lenient than other recording mediums. Optimum temperature is anywhere between 4 degrees and 100 degrees F. (but 41 to 90 degrees F. for unrecorded CDs). Relative humidity can be anywhere between 5 and 90 percent before damage will occur. (Personally, I would never allow mine to get that hot or humid.) Light, however, is damaging to CDs, and can cause warping or shrinking if it gets too intense.

When labeling a disc for identification purposes, write only on the label, screen-printed side using an archival photo marking pen or other soft permanent marker. *Never* use a ball-point or hard pen. It may damage the recording.

If properly cared for, CDs should last for more than a

hundred years. This, however, is an estimate from manufacturers. I've found no exact data from experts on the subject.

Computer diskette media. The number-one problem with computer disks is debris on the drive heads. The debris scratches the coating of the disk. Completely clean the drive every twenty to forty hours of use.

The temperature and humidity requirements for computer diskettes are much the same as for CDs, more flexible than most other recording media. Relative humidity between 8 and 90 percent is fine. Temperature can range from 40 to 120 degrees F. (Again, I wouldn't want mine that hot or humid.) If a disk gets colder than the 40 degrees, allow it to warm up to room temperature before accessing it.

A 3½-inch diskette has a sliding media cover. When the disk is inserted into your computer, this cover slides over to expose the magnetic surface. Leave this cover alone—never touch it with your hands—so debris will not affect your disk. The 5¼-inch floppy diskettes have no cover over the media area at all, so be extra careful. Oils, smudges, and fingerprints from your hands can be damaging to the diskette and data.

Some diskettes also have a write-protection mechanism like the erasure tab on cassette tapes. When the tab is slid down to cover the hole, you cannot record onto that disk. (Follow the instructions for each kind of diskette.) Important disks should be protected in this way to prevent the possibility of accidents.

Disks should be given the same care as other magnetic media. Refer to Chapter 10, "Audio and Video Recordings," for cautions on how magnetic contact can affect a disk.

If you have a properly aligned, clean disk drive and appropriate temperature and humidity, your disks can last for 10 million passes before there is any magnetic deterioration.

Staying Current

With the rapid development of computer technology, it is important to keep your valuable files current. For example, a precious history preserved on a 5¼-inch floppy disk is no good to our descendants if they cannot find a computer with a 5¼-inch drive.

A friend of ours had a TRS 80 computer. (Let me give you an idea of how old and outdated this computer is: There is one on display at the Smithsonian!) His grandfather wrote his personal history on that computer. Unfortunately, the history was never printed out or backed up in any other way. When the computer became obsolete, the family gave it away. Then, recently this old formatted disk showed up, and my friend has no way to read it. Hence, the *big rule* with computers: when you upgrade your computer system, upgrade your disks as well. It's easy and inexpensive to do, and it will help ensure that your data will last your lifetime and beyond.

CONCLUSION

Your life is worth remembering!

I hope you have been convinced that record keeping is an important endeavor. I also hope that you have been able to see that there are many ways to keep records. Surely there are ways that I haven't even mentioned. The most important point that I want to make is that you need to do *something* to preserve your life, traditions, keepsakes, and memories. Your life is important. You are worth remembering.

When I was compiling histories for the Primary and Relief Society General Boards, many miracles occurred. These are personal and sacred to me. But I want to bear witness that I know from my own experiences that we are to keep records.

Writing this book has been another strong indicator to me that we should keep records. The fact that this book is here for you to read is a miracle. I know that it was written solely that others may be motivated to keep records.

Many miracles happened when I was writing this book. One that I'd like to share deals with the photography chapter. I hadn't written anything on the book for a long time. The last thing I had done was to type in PHOTOGRAPHS, SLIDES, AND NEGATIVES and then save the title and take a break. I was procrastinating because I knew that chapter would take a lot of work! Things were busy in my life and I was getting frustrated about writing. The longer I stayed away from writing, the harder it was to be motivated to get back to it. The hardest part was getting started on a chapter—I knew that once I got going I would be fine. I sat down wearily one day, pulled up the photography file, and was shocked to find that three pages had already been written. They were clearly my words, but I had no memory of writing them. How they got there, I'll never know. It was the "jump start" I needed to get going.

I know that if we embark on any record-keeping endeavor, miracles will come our way and we will be blessed beyond measure. The Lord would never ask us to do anything that wouldn't be for our benefit. The scriptures and words from latter-day prophets are full of admonitions to be a record-keeping people. We need to follow their counsel and *do it!*

President Kimball is my exemplar in record keeping. I share his feelings and can't express them better than he did: "Let us then continue on in this important work of recording the things we do, the things we say, the things we think, to be in accordance with the instructions of the Lord. For those of you who may not have already started your books of remembrance and your records, we would suggest that this very day you begin to write your records quite fully and completely. We hope that you will do this, our brothers and sisters, for this is what the Lord has commanded" (*The Teachings of Spencer W. Kimball* [Salt Lake City: Bookcraft, 1982], p. 349).

APPENDIX
WHERE TO FIND THINGS
OR GO FOR HELP

Scrapbook, Journal, and History Supplies

For acid-free, buffered paper, archival sheet protectors, archival corners, tape, pens, binders, templates, scissors, pH testing pens, stickers, and frames, my favorite place is:

> Keeping Memories Alive
> (Formerly known as "The Annex")
> P.O. Box 768
> 260 North Main
> Spanish Fork, UT 84660–0768
> Phone: 1-800-419–4949
> Fax: (801) 798–3420
> Internet: http://www.scrapbooks.com

Call for a distributor in your area, or to have items shipped directly to you.

Audio, Video, and Computers

When you have questions regarding your recorders, tapes, disks, or computers, it is best to call the manufacturer of the individual item. Check a local audio-video store for the toll-free number to call for your particular product.

Conservation Materials for Keepsakes

For acid-free tissue paper, textile roll tubes, archival tape, boxes, encapsulation Mylar, acid-free mat boards, deacidification sprays, photo mounting, archival storage sleeves, envelopes, and boxes for photographic materials, wheat starch, and other supplies:

University Products
517 Main Street
P.O. Box 101
Holyoke, MA 01041–0101
To order: 1–800–628–1912
Customer service and questions: 1–800–762–1165
Fax: 1–800–532–9281
Internet: http//www.university products.com

The Archival Company
Division of University Products
P.O. Box 1239
Northampton, MA 01061–1239
Phone: 1–800–442–7576
Fax: 1–800–532–9281
Internet: http//www.archivalco.com

Light Impressions
439 Monroe Avenue
P.O. Box 940
Rochester, NY 14603–0940
Phone: 1–800–828–6216
Fax: 1–800–828–5539

Cookbooks

To professionally compile your family cookbook, write or call one of the following:

Walter's Publishing
215 5th Avenue S.E.
Waseca, MN 56093
1–800–447–3274

Cookbook Publishers, Inc.
13550 W. 108th St.
P.O. Box 12918
Lenexa, KS 66212

Photographs

Most film boxes have toll-free numbers you can call if you have questions. I have found Konica to be most helpful with inquiries. For information regarding photos put onto computer disks, or any other photo finishing questions, call:

1–800–95-KONICA

They will help you locate a dealer in your area or will fill mail orders.

Heirlooms

For information on heirloom conservation, contact:

American Institute for Conservation of Historic
    and Artistic Works (AIC)
1717 K Street NW Suite #301
Washington, DC 20006
(202) 452-9545

Call or send for a catalogue that will refer you to conservators in your area.

Genealogical Information

National Genealogical Society
4527 17th Street North
Arlington, VA 22207
(703) 525–0050

To find a genealogical society in your area, send a self-addressed, stamped envelope to:

Federation of Genealogical Societies
P.O. Box 220
Davenport, IA 52805

Professional Researchers

Lists of professional researchers are available at the Family History Library in Salt Lake City or from the Board for Certification of Genealogists.
Write to:

Board for Certification of Genealogists
P.O. Box 5816
Falmouth, VA 22403

National Archives

The National Archives has millions of documents on microfilm, including ship arrival lists, census records, military records, and federal land grant records. Forms from the National Archives can help you purchase microfilms or request photocopies of specific records. Many of the records at the Archives are available at the LDS Church's Family History Library or other major libraries.

The main branch of the Archives is in Washington, D.C., but there are regional offices throughout the United States.

Main Branch
Eighth Street and Pennsylvania, NW
Washington, DC 20408

New England Region
380 Trapelo Road
Waltham, MA 02154
States served: CT, MA, ME, NH, RI, VT
Phone: (617) 647–8100

Northeast Region
Building 22, MOT
Bayonne, NJ 07002–5388
States served: NJ, NY, Puerto Rico, the Virgin Islands
Phone: (201) 823–7252

Mid-Atlantic Region
9th and Market Streets, Room 1350
Philadelphia, PA 19107
States served: DC, DE, MD, PA, VA, WV
Phone: (215) 597–3000

Southeast Region
1557 St. Joseph Avenue
East Point, GA 30344
States served: AL, FL, GA, KY, MS, NC, SC, TN
Phone: (404) 763–7477

Great Lakes Region
7358 South Pulaski Road
Chicago, IL 60629
States served: IL, IN, MI, MN, OH, WI
Phone: (312) 581–7816

Central Plains Region
2312 East Bannister Road
Kansas City, MO 64131
States served: IA, KS, MO, NE
Phone: (816) 926–6272

Southwest Region
501 West Felix Street
P.O. Box 6216
Fort Worth, TX 76115
States served: AR, LA, NM, OK, TX
Phone: (817) 334–5525

Rocky Mountain Region
Building 48, Denver Federal Center
Denver, CO 80225
States served: CO, MT, ND, SD, UT, WY
Phone: (303) 236–0817

Pacific Southwest Region
24000 Avila Road
Laguna Niguel, CA 92677
States served: AZ; Southern California counties of Imperial,
    Inyo, Kern, Los Angeles, Orange, Riverside, San
    Bernadino, San Diego, San Luis Obispo, Santa Barbara,
    and Ventura; Nevada's Clark County
Phone: (714) 643–4241

Pacific Sierra Region
1000 Commodore Drive
San Bruno, CA 94066
States served: CA (except southern counties covered under
    Pacific Southwest Region), HI, NV (except Clark
    County), and the Pacific Ocean area
Phone: (415) 876–9009

Pacific Northwest Region
6125 Sand Point Way NE
Seattle, WA 98115
States served: ID, OR, WA
Phone: (206) 526–6507

Alaska Region
654 West Third Avenue
Anchorage, AK 99501
State served: AK
Phone: (907) 271–2441

Genealogy Libraries

When requesting any research or information, make your letters brief and specific. Enclose a self-addressed, stamped envelope. A fee will be required for photocopies; send a check or money order, or ask whether they can bill you.

Family History Library
The Church of Jesus Christ of Latter-day Saints
35 North West Temple
Salt Lake City, UT 84150
(801) 240–2331
Call for information regarding a family history center in your area.

Library of Congress
Thomas Jefferson Building
10 First Street, SE
Washington, DC 20540

Library, National Society of the
Daughters of the American Revolution
1776 D Street, NW
Washington, DC 20006

New England Historic Genealogical Society
101 Newbury Street
Boston, MA 02116

Western Reserve Historical Society
10825 East Boulevard
Cleveland, OH 44106

Los Angeles Public Library
630 West Fifth Street
Los Angeles, CA 90071

New York Public Library
U.S. History, Local History, and Genealogy Division
Fifth Avenue and 42nd Street
New York, NY 10018

Newberry Library
60 West Walton Street
Chicago, IL 60610

Allen County Public Library
P.O. Box 2270
900 Webster Street
Fort Wayne, IN 46801

Passenger Ship Lists

If your ancestors arrived in the United States by ship between 1820 and 1950, a copy of the ship's manifest can be obtained. These include such information as age, gender, occupation, and country of origin of each passenger. You will need to know the person's name, where he or she arrived, and the month and year of arrival. Send a self-addressed, stamped envelope to:

National Archives
General Reference Branch
NNRG, 8th and Pennsylvania Ave. NW
Washington, DC 20408

Ask for the NATF Form 81. There is a small fee.

Military Records

Even if your ancestor never served in the military, there may be draft records under his or her name.

If you are seeking information from before 1917, send a self-addressed, stamped envelope to:

General Reference Branch (NNRG-P)
National Archives and Records Administration
7th and Pennsylvania Ave. NW
Washington, DC 20408

Ask for the NATF Form 80, Order and Billing for Copies of Veterans Records.

For 1917 draft registration records, send a self-addressed, stamped envelope to:

National Archives
Atlanta Branch
1557 St. Joseph Avenue
East Point, GA 30344

Ask for a World War I Registration Card request form.

For military records after 1917, send a self-addressed, stamped envelope to:

National Personnel Records Center (MPR)
9700 Page Boulevard
St. Louis, MO 63132

Ask for NA Form 13043.

Land Grants

Some of our ancestors received land grants from the federal government. For information, send a self-addressed, stamped envelope to:

National Archives
Reference Branch NNRR
Washington, DC 20409

Include ancestor's full name, the state where the land was granted, and if it was before or after 1908.

Vital Records

The booklet "Where to Write for Vital Records: Births, Deaths, Marriages, and Divorces" (Hyattsville, Maryland: U.S. Department of Health and Human Services) lists every state in the United States and where to find birth, marriage, divorce, and death records. If your library doesn't have this booklet, you can purchase it. Send a self-addressed, stamped envelope to:

Superintendent of Documents
U.S. Government Printing Office
Washington, DC 20402

Following is a current (as of this writing) list of places you can contact to obtain vital records. There is a small charge for locating and sending information.

Alabama
Center for Health Statistics
State Department of Public Health
434 Monroe Street
Montgomery, AL 36130–1701

Alaska
Department of Health and Social Services
Bureau of Vital Statistics
P.O. Box H-02G
Juneau, AK 99811–0675

Arizona
Vital Records Section
Arizona Department of Health Services
P.O. Box 3887
Phoenix, AZ 85030

Arkansas
Division of Vital Records
Arkansas Department of Health
4815 West Markham Street
Little Rock, AR 72201

California
Vital Statistics Section
Department of Health Services
410 N Street
Sacramento, CA 95814

Colorado
Vital Records Section
Colorado Department of Health
4210 East 11th Avenue
Denver, CO 80220

Connecticut
Vital Records
Department of Health Services
150 Washington Street
Hartford, CT 06106

Delaware
Office of Vital Statistics
Division of Public Health
P.O. Box 637
Dover, DE 19903

District of Columbia
Vital Records Branch
Room 3009
425 I Street, NW
Washington, DC 20001

Florida
Department of Health and Rehabilitative Services
Office of Vital Statistics
1217 Pearl Street
Jacksonville, FL 32202

Georgia
Georgia Department of Human Resources
Vital Records Unit
Room 217-H
47 Trinity Avenue, SW
Atlanta, GA 30334

Hawaii
Office of Health Status Monitoring
State Department of Health
P.O. Box 3378
Honolulu, HI 96801

Idaho
Vital Statistics Unit
Idaho Department of Health and Welfare
450 West State Street
Statehouse Mail
Boise, ID 83720–9990

Illinois
Division of Vital Records
Illinois Department of Public Health
605 West Jefferson Street
Springfield, IL 62702–5079

Indiana
Vital Records Section
State Board of Health
1330 West Michigan Street
P.O. Box 1964
Indianapolis, IN 46206–1964

Iowa
Iowa Department of Public Health
Vital Records Section
Lucas Office Building
321 East 12th Street
Des Moines, IA 50319

Kansas
Office of Vital Statistics
Kansas State Department of Health and Environment
900 Jackson Street
Topeka, KS 66612–1290

Kentucky
Office of Vital Statistics
Department for Health Services
275 East Main Street
Frankfort, KY 40621

Louisiana
Vital Records Registry
Office of Public Health
325 Loyola Avenue
New Orleans, LA 70112

Maine
Office of Vital Records
Human Services Building
Station 11
State House
Augusta, ME 04333

Maryland
Division of Vital Records
Department of Health and Mental Hygiene
Metro Executive Building
4201 Patterson Avenue
P.O. Box 68760
Baltimore, MD 21215–0020

Massachusetts
Registry of Vital Records and Statistics
150 Tremont Street, Room B-3
Boston, MA 02111

Michigan
Office of the State Registrar and Center for Health Statistics
Michigan Department of Public Health
3423 North Logan Street
Lansing, MI 48909

Minnesota
Minnesota Department of Health
Section of Vital Statistics
717 Delaware Street, SE
P.O. Box 9441
Minneapolis, MN 55440

Mississippi
Vital Records
State Department of Health
2423 North State Street
Jackson, MS 39216

Missouri
Department of Health
Bureau of Vital Records
1730 East Elm
P.O. Box 570
Jefferson City, MO 65102

Montana
Bureau of Records and Statistics
State Department of Health and Environmental Sciences
Helena, MT 59620

Nebraska
Bureau of Vital Statistics
State Department of Health
301 Centennial Mall South
P.O. Box 95007
Lincoln, NE 68509–5007

Nevada
Division of Health—Vital Statistics
Capitol Complex
505 East King Street #102
Carson City, NV 89710

New Hampshire
Bureau of Vital Records
Health and Human Services Building
6 Hazen Drive
Concord, NH 03301

New Jersey
State Department of Health
Bureau of Vital Statistics CN 370
South Warren and Market Streets
Trenton, NJ 08625

New Mexico
Vital Statistics
New Mexico Health Services Division
1190 St. Francis Drive
Santa Fe, NM 87503

New York (except New York City)
Vital Records Section
State Department of Health
Empire State Plaza
Tower Building
Albany, NY 12237–0023

New York City
Bureau of Vital Records
Department of Health of New York City
125 Worth Street
New York, NY 10013

North Carolina
Department of Environment, Health, and Natural Resources
Division of Epidemiology
Vital Records Section
225 North McDowell Street
P.O. Box 27687
Raleigh, NC 27611–7687

North Dakota
Division of Vital Records
State Capitol
600 East Boulevard Avenue
Bismarck, ND 58505

Ohio
Division of Vital Statistics
Ohio Department of Health
G-20 Ohio Department Building
65 South Front Street
Columbus, OH 43266–0333

Oklahoma
Vital Records Section
State Department of Health
1000 Northeast 10th Street
P.O. Box 53551
Oklahoma City, OK 73152

Oregon
Oregon Health Division
Vital Statistics Section
P.O. Box 116
Portland, OR 97207

Pennsylvania
Division of Vital Records
State Department of Health
Central Building
101 South Mercer Street
P.O. Box 1528
New Castle, PA 16103

Puerto Rico
Department of Health
Demographic Registry
P.O. Box 11854
Fernandez Juncos Station
San Juan, PR 00910

Rhode Island
Division of Vital Records
Rhode Island Department of Health
Room 101, Cannon Building
3 Capitol Hill
Providence, RI 02908–5097

South Carolina
Office of Vital Records and Public Health Statistics
South Carolina Department of Health and
    Environmental Control
2600 Bull Street
Columbia, SC 29201

South Dakota
State Department of Health
Center for Health Policy and Statistics
Vital Records
523 E. Capitol
Pierre, SD 57501

Tennessee
Tennessee Vital Records
Department of Health and Environment
Cordell Hull Building
Nashville, TN 37219–5402

Texas
Bureau of Vital Statistics
Texas Department of Health
1100 West 49th Street
Austin, TX 78756–3191

Utah
Bureau of Vital Records
Utah Department of Health
288 North 1460 West
P.O. Box 16700
Salt Lake City, UT 84116–0700

Vermont
Vermont Department of Health
Vital Records Section
Box 70
60 Main Street
Burlington, VT 05402
(or, for records prior to 1955:)
Division of Public Records
6 Baldwin Street
Montpelier, VT 05602

Virginia
Division of Vital Records
State Health Department
P.O. Box 1000
Richmond, VA 23208–1000

Washington
Vital Records
1112 South Quince
P.O. Box 9709, ET-11
Olympia, WA 98504–9709

West Virginia
Vital Registration Office
Division of Health
State Capitol Complex Bldg. 3
Charleston, WV 25305

Wisconsin
Vital Records
1 West Wilson Street
P.O. Box 309
Madison, WI 53701

Wyoming
Vital Records Services
Hathaway Building
Cheyenne, WY 82002

GLOSSARY

A.N.S.I. American National Standards Institute. This organization establishes standards for materials and practices for anything from electric power lines to paper and ink.

accelerated aging test. Simulates the natural aging process on material samples, using elevated temperature and humidity.

acetate. Material that combines cellulose, acetic, and sulfuric acids; used in various products, including photographic films and packaging sheets. *Tri*-acetates are archival; *di*-acetates are not.

acid. A chemical substance capable of forming hydrogen ions when dissolved in water. Acids can weaken cellulose in paper, wood products, and cloth, making them brittle. They may be introduced in paper manufacturing and left in intentionally (as in certain sizings) or incidentally (as with insufficient bleaching). Acids may also be introduced by migration from other materials or from atmospheric pollution.

acid migration. Transfer of acid from an acidic material to a less acidic or pH-neutral material. For example, acid migration can occur in books when acid from boards, end papers, protective tissues, or paper covers transfers to the text paper.

acid-free. Materials that have a pH of 7.0 or higher. The term is often used incorrectly as a synonym for *alkaline* or *buffered*. Acid-free materials may be produced from any cellulose fiber source (such as cotton or wood) if (1) acid is eliminated from the bleaching process and aluminum sulfate from sizing; or (2) the materials are buffered with an alkaline substance to prevent acid formation from air pollutants.

acrylic. A particular type of plastic important in preservation because of its stability (resistence to change over time), a feature *not* common to all plastics. Other noted characteristics are its transparency, light weight, weather resistance, colorfastness, and rigidity. Acrylics are available in sheets, films, and resin adhesives. Perspex, Lucite, and Plexiglas are common trade names for the sheet form.

albumen prints. A photographic printing process especially popular from the 1850s through the 1890s, using egg whites (albumen) instead of gelatin (used currently) to form the emulsion.

alkali. A caustic substance having a pH above 7.0, capable of neutralizing acid.

alkaline. Substances that have a pH over 7.0; added to material to neutralize acids. Also used as an alkaline buffer or reserve to counteract future acid formation. An alkaline can be added during either the manufacturing or deacidification process.

alkaline reserve. Buffer or reserve of an alkaline substance added to paper to counteract acid—usually 3 percent precipitated calcium or magnesium carbonate by paper weight.

alum. Aluminum sulfate used with rosin to size paper, making it water resistant. Alum-sized paper is acidic and therefore *not* archival.

archival or **archivally sound**. A nontechnical term suggesting a material or product is permanent, durable, or chemically stable and therefore can safely be used in preservation procedures. The phrase is not quantifiable, and no standards exist that define how long an "archival" or "archivally sound" material will last. The term also refers to preservation or storage procedures that are reversible and do not permanently alter an artifact.

buffering. The addition of alkaline agents such as calcium or magnesium carbonate during the paper-making process to counteract acidic contamination. The degree of buffering (usually 2 to 3 percent) is measured by the weight of the paper. *See also* alkaline.

calcium carbonate. An alkaline chemical used as a buffer in papers and boards.

cellulose, cellulose fiber. Cellulose is the main element in the cell wall of plants. Its fiber is the primary component of paper, obtained by separating the nonfibrous elements from such sources as wood, woody plants, and cotton, and then bleaching the remaining fiber in the pulping process.

conservation. Treating library or archive works of art, museum objects, or materials to stabilize them chemically and strengthen them physically, thus preserving them as long as possible in their original form.

conservator. Person responsible for care, restoration, and repair of museum articles.

deacidification. A chemical treatment that (1) neutralizes acid in a material such as paper and (2) deposits an alkaline buffer to prevent future acid attack. Although this treatment does increase stability, it cannot restore strength or flexibility to brittle materials.

emulsion. In photography, a single or multilayered coating (made from gelatin or some other material) deposited on a film, glass, or paper support; it carries light- or radio-sensitive chemicals (usually silver halides). These chemicals create a latent image upon exposure that, when developed, produces a visible image.

encapsulation. A form of protective enclosure for papers and other flat objects. In polyester encapsulation, an item is placed between two sheets of transparent polyester film. These sheets are then sealed along the edges (often with an acid-free tape). The item is now physically supported and protected from the atmosphere, though it can continue to deteriorate inside the capsule. Because it is not adhered to the sheets, the item can be removed simply by cutting one edge of the capsule.

ferrotype. (1) The appearance of shiny patches on the gelatin surface of photographs, caused by contact with a smooth surface (particularly plastic enclosures or glass) in high relative humidity. If photos are stored in plastic enclosures under pressure (such as in a stack), ferrotyping can occur at moderate levels of relative humidity. (2) A finishing process involving heat, pressure, and a polished metal sheet while drying fiber-based black-and-white prints, creating a highly glossed surface.

fiber content. A description of the types and percentages of fibers found in paper, board, or cloth. This is important because the quality of the fiber significantly affects both the durability and the chemical stability of the item.

fixer. A solution that removes unexposed silver halides (light-sensitive metallic compounds) from a photo's emulsion, making the image stable and impervious to white light. The time the emulsion spends in the fixer (or "hypo") is called the "clearing" time.

foxing. Spots of various sizes and intensity (usually brownish) that disfigure paper; caused by a combination of fungi, paper impurities, and dampness.

fungus. Parasitic lower plants that grow by absorbing dissolved organic matter. They include molds, mildew, smuts, mushrooms, and yeasts.

gelatin. A binder made from animal parts, used as a support for the light-sensitive particles in certain photographic emulsions.

231

glazing. Glass or other transparent material used for framing (as well as for windows).

ground wood pulp. Pulp composed of ground-up wood, typically found in grey cardboard or brown corrugated board (box board). Ground wood pulp is nonarchival and acidic because it is quickly and economically processed, leaving most of the harmful impurities (largely lignin) in the pulp.

hinge. A small piece of linen tape or other neutral material (such as mulberry paper), folded in half and glued to a piece of artwork and its backing. Occasionally it is laid unfolded across the top edge of the art and onto the backing. The term can also refer to a strip of tape used to join the mat to a backing piece of board to create a folder mat.

hinging papers. An archival hinging system that attaches artwork to an album page or mounting board. Typically, lightweight but strong Japanese papers of various weights combined with organic and reversible adhesives (such as wheat or rice starch paste) are used.

humidity. The moisture condition of the air. The term *relative humidity* refers to the percentage of air moisture relative to the amount that air can retain at any given temperature without precipitation.

hygrometer. An instrument that measures the relative humidity of the air.

hypo. Originally an abbreviation for sodium hyposulfate, it now refers to sodium thiosulfate (the chemical used in fixing baths to remove unexposed silver halides from silver emulsion film). It more generally refers to a fixer solution that may also contain certain acids and/or hardening agents.

kraft paper. The common brown wrapping paper used by most businesses, which comes in rolls and is sold by weight and width (in inches). A strong, tough paper, made entirely from wood pulp, it probably has a high acid content.

lamination. A process that reinforces fragile paper, usually with thin, translucent or transparent sheets. An unacceptable conservation method, lamination can potentially cause damage from high heat and pressure during application, unstable materials, or difficulty in removing the laminated item, especially long after the application.

litmus paper. Chemically treated paper, sensitive to pH. Blue litmus paper turns red if exposed to acid; red litmus paper turns blue if exposed to alkali.

museum board. Mat board that is 100 percent cotton as well as acid- and lignin-free, having a uniform color throughout. It is sometimes lumped together with conservator's mat board, which is *not* 100 percent cotton, but is acid- and lignin-free.

negative. Developed film that has a reversed-tone image of an object. Light areas of the image are heavy or dark with silver deposits, and dark areas of the image are light or transparent. When negative images are printed on paper or film, they turn "positive" and look like the original object.

neutral pH. A rating of 7.0 on the pH scale, exhibiting neither acid nor alkaline (base) qualities. Paper and board stock with a neutral pH are recommended as storage or mounting materials for photographs.

nonaqueous. Solution that does not contain water or is not water-based.

nonarchival. Will not protect item from deterioration due to aging. Nonarchival products break down, deteriorate, and have adverse affects on items they touch. The term also refers to procedures that are not reversible, permanently altering the artifact.

nonbleeding. Materials that show no signs of dye or pigment transfer from one to another while in damp contact and under pressure for a specified time period (usually 48 hours).

nonbuffered. Paper pulp that is not infused with buffering agents such as calcium carbonate. Some buffering agents have adverse affects on various types of photographic prints.

nonporous. Having no absorbent qualities.

nonreversible. Permanent. A nonarchival procedure that uses permanent adhesive or a mounting technique that will not permit original artifact to be removed without damage.

oxidation. To combine with oxygen; a chemical reaction that converts an element into its oxide. Image silver can react chemically with oxidizing agents, resulting in the discoloration of photographs.

parchment. Once made from animal skins, parchment papers today are manufactured from cellulose fibers. Unsized stock is bathed in sulfuric acid to give it an aged, authentic look. Papers today have extremely hard surfaces, high wet-strength, and resistance to grease and dirt.

Photographic Activity Test (P.A.T.). Accelerated aging test used to simulate the natural aging process and thus test the archival quality of various papers and paper products. A specialized photo emulsion is applied to a paper sample at elevated temperature and humidity levels.

pigment. Particles used to give color, body, or opacity to a semiliquid artist's material.

plasticizer. A chemical added to plastic resins that enhances flexibility, workability, or stretching capacity. Plastic enclosures should not be used to store photos, because plasticizers tend to become volatile and can cause damage.

Plexiglas. Trade name for acrylic sheet material made by Rohn and Haas. *See also* acrylic.

polyester. Common name for polyethylene terephthalate plastic. It is transparent and colorless and has high tensile strength. Because it is also chemically stable, it is useful in preservation, and is generally used in sheet or film form to make folders, encapsulations, and book jackets. Its thickness is often measured in mils. Popular trade names are Mylar, by Dupont, and Mellinex, by ICI.

polyethylene. A chemically stable, highly flexible, transparent or translucent plastic with a low melting point. When made with no surface coatings or additives, it is useful as a sleeve protector for photographic preservation.

polypropylene. A stiff, heat-resistant, chemically stable plastic, with better clarity than polyethylene and less static charge than polyester. This is a good plastic for preservation when made into sleeves or containers for photos, slides, or film.

polyvinyl acetate (PVA). A colorless, transparent plastic generally used in adhesives, which are themselves referred to as "PVA" or "PVA adhesives." There are dozens of such adhesives; those which are "internally plasticized" are more chemically stable and suitable for preservation.

polyvinyl chloride (PVC). A plastic less chemically stable than others, which can emit damaging hydrochloric acid as it deteriorates. It therefore has limited use in preservation techniques. Some plastics called "vinyl" may actually be PVC.

preservation. Maintaining objects in their original condition through retention, proper care, and restoration (if necessary). Also refers to activities associated with library, archival, or museum artifact maintenance.

pulp. Cellulose fiber from which paper and paperboard are manufactured by either mechanical or chemical means. Sources of cellulose fiber include wood, cotton, straw, jute, bagasse, bamboo, hemp, various leaf fibers, and reeds.

purified wood pulp. Pulp processed from wood chips and then broken down into concentrated alpha cellulose fibers. Impurities (such as acidic lignin) are then removed by bleaching, making the pulp suitable for use in archival paper stock.

rag content. Measurement applied to paper that is made chiefly from linen or cotton fibers instead of highly acidic wood pulp. High rag content usually indicates a neutral pH.

rag paper. Cotton fiber paper made from cotton cuttings and linters.

RC. Stands for "resin coated." Photographic prints or papers that are resin coated are less expensive and easier to process and wash than gelatin silver bromide/chloride emulsions, but they are *not archival*.

relative humidity. The ratio between the quantity of water vapor present in the air and the quantity that would saturate that air at any given temperature.

restoration. Procedures that bring back a damaged object as close as possible to its original condition.

rosin. An acidic—and hence nonarchival—internal sizing for paper.

sizings. Chemicals added to paper, making it less absorbent so inks that are applied won't bleed. Acidic sizings (rosin and alum) can foster damage and deterioration; other sizings are not acidic and are more chemically stable.

spores. A walled, single- or multi-celled, reproductive body of an organism produced by plants and some invertebrates..

ultraviolet (UV) light. Electromagnetic radiation having a wavelength beyond the visible part of violet in the spectrum. Sunlight and fluorescent light are common sources of UV light. It can be damaging to items meant to be preserved.

UV filter. A material used to filter out the ultraviolet (UV) rays of visible light. UV light is potentially damaging to library, archival, and museum objects; its removal from storage, use, and exhibition spaces can reduce the rate of deterioration of library materials. UV light is more prevalent in sunlight and fluorescent lights than incandescent lights. Filtering material is usually placed over windows or fluorescent light tubes, over glass used in framing, or in exhibition cases.

vellum. The term originally referred to calfskin that was cleaned, preserved by soaking in lime solution, dried, stretched, scraped, and polished, then used for writing, printing, or binding. It now refers to a smooth paper finish.

vinyl. A word imprecisely used to refer to a variety of plastics, many of which are not archivally sound. For safe plastics, see listings for polyester, polypropylene, polyvinyl acetate, and acrylic.

wood pulp. Pulp from various types of trees used to manufacture paper. There are two basic kinds: (1) the mechanically processed pulp or ground wood from which newsprint is made, and (2) chemically processed pulp, which is a higher grade since more impurities (such as lignin) are removed.

BIBLIOGRAPHY

Church of Jesus Christ of Latter-day Saints. "Discovering Your Family Tree." Salt Lake City, 1993.

———. Homemaking Booklet. Salt Lake City, 1981.

Daughters of Utah Pioneers. "Preserving Pioneer Relics." Salt Lake City, 1984.

Eastman Kodak Company. "Conservation of Photographs." 1985.

Historic New Orleans Collection. Preservation Guides 1–6.

Keefe, Laurence E., and Dennis Inch. *The Life of a Photograph*. Woburn, Massachusetts: Butterworth Publishers, 1984.

Lawrence, Priscilla O'Reilly. "Before Disaster Strikes." Louisiana: The Historic New Orleans Collection, 1992.

National Committee to Save America's Cultural Collections, comp. *Caring for Your Collections: Preserving and Protecting Your Art and Other Collectibles*. New York: Harry N. Abrams, Inc., 1992.

Plummer, Louise. *Thoughts of a Grasshopper.* Salt Lake City: Deseret Book, 1992.

Polk, Timothy W. *How to Outlive Your Lifetime.* Sunnyvale, California: Family Life International, 1994.

Tuttle, Craig A. *An Ounce of Preservation: A Guide to the Care of Papers and Photographs.* Highland City, Florida: Rainbow Books, 1995.

U.S. Government Printing Office. "Family Folklore." 1990.

Wilhelm, Henry. *The Permanence and Care of Color Photographs: Traditional and Digital Color Prints, Color Negatives, Slides, and Motion Pictures.* Grinnell, Iowa: Preservation Publishing Company, 1993.

Wolfman, Ira. *Do People Grow on Family Trees? Genealogy for Kids and Other Beginners.* New York: Workman Publishing Company, Inc., 1991.

INDEX